What a fantastic read! This book is a ...... with ...... anticipation for God-promises to b ...... reader. There's practical insight, Godly wisdom, ... released throughout the book that gives and even sows seeds of healing into the reader on every page. A real life-changer for many. This is also a Healing & Deliverance handbook; a must read for anyone wanting to learn more in the exciting field of H. & D.
~Evangelist Jay L. Jellison, Becoming Love Ministries Association, Awaken the Harvest Crusades, and Disciple Topeka.

Suzanne teaches simple but powerful Scripture guided tools to learn how to effectively put on the full armor of God in order to prevent unwanted, take-you-by-surprise enemy attacks. I believe the Lord has anointed this book to bring hope and healing to those all over the world who do not believe hope is possible.
~Laura Corbin

This book, *Good Grief ~ I'm Healed,* is a must read! Our Father desires everyone to be healed and this will begin the journey for you.
~Evangelist Chad Seabright, Co-Director, City Taker Training Center (CTTC), [citytakerstrainingcenter.com]

Grief is a journey to be taken hand-in-hand with the Savior. He desires truth in our inward parts. Suzanne warmly and joyfully invites you to walk with her through the valley of the shadow of mental distress to experience the Lord's nearness, provision and deliverance through it all. With personal examples of victory and Spirit-filled exhortation, this encouraging testimony will help you better steward your mind-body connection as you deepen your relationship with Christ.
~Elizabeth Fischborn

Good Grief ~ I'm Healed is truly destined to change lives. Everything from the raw and honest sharing, to the practical prayers, and tips to walk through your own journey, this book is hands down a must read for anyone!
~Dawn Hill, Founder, Faith Voyager Ministries

In reading through *Good Grief ~ I'm Healed,* it is clear that God has guided Suzanne and is using her to share His truths. She was bold in writing this and has provided some very relatable and practical steps in order to take away the power that the devil grasps at in our minds.
~Megan Sinkler

No doubt, the raw emotion of Suzanne's personal journey inspires us all to great hope as we recognize this: what the enemy meant to destroy, in each of our lives, God can and will use for good. He longs to resurrect beauty from ashes and nothing is more evident in Suzanne's journey than this truth.
~Christy Austin, MA, LPCC, Founder, Healing Talk LLC
[healingtalk.online],
President, Enkindle Ministries [enkindleministries.com]

GOOD GRIEF

I'M HEALED

Suzanne Grimaud

GOOD GRIEF

GRIEF

I'M HEALED

"Hurt in the World, Healed by the Word"

CEDAR GATE PUBLISHING

Proof and Copyeditor: Megan Sinkler

Content editors: Jay Jellison and Dawn Hill

Cover design: Scott Soliz @Zeal Desiño Studio

Author photo photo by Perillaproductions (Andres Perilla)

softcover: ISBN: 978-1-7363916-0-0

ebook: ISBN: 978-1-7363916-1-7

Printed in the United States of America

DEDICATION

This work from my heart is dedicated to the ones dearest to my heart, my family.

To my best friend and husband, Greg:

Thank you for encouraging me, cheering me on and for your constant love and support. I love you dearly!

To our adult children, Alana, Danica and Garrison:

*Thank you for believing in your mom. I believe in you too!
If you dream it, I know you'll do it!
I love you!*

Special honorable dedication: Rev. Ron Frizzell

*Thank you, Ron, for providing the missing key to my inner healing.
Your sacrifice of time and ministry just a couple of weeks before your journey to heaven will surely continue to produce healing fruit for many people, for years to come.
I am eternally grateful for you and thankful the Lord used you in my life.*

TABLE OF CONTENTS

FOREWORD

The emotional healing in this book is tangible! As I read Suzanne's words, I was blown away by the refreshing waves of peace I felt in the depths of my own soul. The content conveys incredible knowledge and tools, but there's also a substantial supernatural healing that occurs through reading her words.

I first met Suzanne many years ago at our ministry's annual Board Retreat in Georgia. Her joyful zeal struck a chord in my heart, and I found myself drawn to her expressive art of communication. It's simply contagious. From baking to teaching (and everything in between), I've seen Suzanne creatively serve many. Over the years, I've been deeply challenged by her boldness to share her faith in the midst of everyday circumstances. No one is overlooked when she's around including cashiers, policemen, and parking lot attendants. She loves well.

As a Licensed Professional Clinical Counselor for many years, I've observed a strong need for emotional healing in the Body of Christ. We as the Church know how to "fan the flame" in others through preaching, worship and prayer but often feel helpless to heal souls. Soul wounds cause deep emotional pain that often manifests physically, and a good sermon alone doesn't fix these deep hurts. Because we are physical, spiritual and emotional beings, each aspect is vital to live the abundant life Jesus Himself promised. What I love about this book is that Suzanne beautifully addresses each area and also shares practical advice to bring healing and wholeness to body, soul, and mind.

When it comes to emotional health, there are not many who are brave enough to vulnerably share "the good, the bad, and the ugly" as as Suzanne does throughout these pages. The throbbing pain :scribes in her darkest days is heartfelt and palpable. She states, emical imbalance literally causes 'dots' to be incorrectly connected in the brain and the emotions will often give away your secret irrational and temporary beliefs." In all reality, due to the fallen nature of our world, we all grapple with aspects of mental and emotional health. No doubt, the raw emotion of Suzanne's personal journey inspires us all to great hope as we recognize this: what the enemy meant to destroy, in each of our lives, God can and will use for good. He longs to resurrect beauty from ashes and nothing is more evident in Suzanne's journey than this truth.

As a therapist, I've had the privilege of walking with many in their darkest hour. I've led group therapy at psychiatric hospitals, conducted countless intakes, helped stabilize crises and processed personal loss with many clients in the privacy of my office. One discovery I've made over the years is that fear is the root of most mental health issues. From panic attacks to phobias, fear is intense and causes us to behave irrationally. Suzanne boldly exposes the lies surrounding fears and equips each reader with practical tools to overcome the most irrational fears and behaviors. "The weapons used against me have always shown up in the form of past fears I have had in my life. The 'fear dot' is then improperly connected in my brain to a 'fact dot' and a lie is unleashed." Everyone can benefit from this message because our world is currently inundated with fear. This is a must read for every believer to confront fear and, once and for all, get rid of those pesky thoughts producing unwanted behaviors.

The keys shared in these pages will bring freedom to many. I'm grateful for the labor of love found in these pages and have no doubt many tears of joy and freedom will trickle down the pages that follow, freeing countless hearts. As Suzanne so eloquently declares, "There are treasures in our trauma when the Lord comes to our rescue. Truth triumphs over trauma!"

—Christy Austin, MA, LPCC
Founder, Healing Talk LLC [healingtalk.online]
President, Enkindle Ministries [enkindleministries.com]

INTRO:
A CALL TO REMEMBER

The summer of 2019 was quite eventful as well as memorable in many ways. While recently rummaging through old journals, I ran across an entry I wrote that warm July that caused me to pause and remember once again. The night before this entry in my prayer journal, Greg and I received a prophetic word given by Shawn Bolz while sitting in a crowd at a conference in Amarillo, Texas. Through this mighty man of God whom we did not personally know, the Lord confirmed what He was already speaking to our hearts—specific words no man would know as some had been uttered in private prayers and not recorded anywhere. Our takeaway echoed our awareness that God sees where we are, knows all the details concerning our lives and He loves to give His children good gifts. It was a gift of love from the Father by use of words from one of His, to another, or in our case, to a pair. Though we too have the ability to hear directly from the Holy Spirit ourselves, as Jesus Christ made that possible for all who believe and receive Him as their Savior, He also speaks to us through the written Word of God and through His sons and daughters' mouths. These rare word gifts are treasures to my heart and worth recalling and remembering.

As referenced in my journal, Greg reminded me of another time the Lord used a man of God to confirm through a freshly spoken word, a written Word the Holy Spirit had whispered personally to me. At a moment when I was in deep sorrow, the Lord offered the gift of hope to my aching heart and drew me to His Word. I remember on Sunday, January 2, 2005, while standing on the platform at church ready to serve on the worship team, our pastor at the time, Rev. David Gallimore, entered the room from the side door with this exclamation, "Church! It is a new year and the Lord has just changed my opening statement to you with a fresh Word I have never opened a New Year's service with before." He continued with *Lamentations 3:22-23 NIV, "Because of the Lord's great love, we are not consumed for His compassions never fail. They are fresh and new every morning; great is your faithfulness!"*

How could Pastor Gallimore have known that we needed to hear this exact passage of scripture? He didn't. He simply heard what the Holy Spirit was saying and then he repeated it. I remember looking straight at Greg and seeing his jaw drop to the floor as he and I locked eyes in wonder, knowing we had just received a personal gift of a Word from the Lord as a sign that I had indeed heard from Him correctly during my lament a few days earlier, just days after Christmas. The Father was letting us know that in my grieving, He heard my cries and in response, hope was in sight for the healing our marriage was receiving.

At my darkest hour, He called my name and led me straight into his loving heart. I remember how God took a hold of me in my brokenness and shined His light on His own Word so He could weep and mourn with me, then remind me that I am His, that I was not forgotten and would be restored. The Holy Spirit drew me close to the Father and allowed me to curl up in His lap and rest in His arms. This encounter has been one I have drawn on time and time again as I remember that He is close to the brokenhearted and He brings healing through His Word. I soon knew he was calling me to be a conduit for his love and mercy, or rather a container for His grace to flow through. He is not looking for perfection but for people He can inhabit to extend His gift of forgiveness through to a world who feels they have no hope.

In spite of my heartaches and in spite of my grief, He has been faithful and has restored what was stolen from me. As Jeremiah said in *Lamentations 3:20-24 NLT, "I will never forget this awful time, as I grieve over my loss. Yet I still dare to hope when I remember this: the un-failing love of the Lord never ends! By his mercies we have been kept from complete destruction. Great is His faithfulness; His mercies begin afresh each day. I say to myself, the Lord is my inheritance; therefore, I will hope in Him!"*

As I remember and reflect back on this monumental time in my life, I am reminded of the recent movie remake of "The Lion King." You might recall when Simba, the prodigal son of the lion tribe, gazed into the reflecting pool and saw the face of his dad, Mufassa, and then heard these words that caused him to rise up and return to the tribe: "Remember who you are!" It was at that moment that strength rose up within him, causing the pride of the pride to sprint home and take his place as The Lion King of the Jungle. Because he remembered who he was as the son of a King, and heir to the throne, his family was saved. The community was saved. The jungle was saved. Water was restored and the enemy was forced to flee. As a result, blessing and favor was given to Simba as he fulfilled his destiny. When Simba remembered who he was and then took action, he was positioned to receive all that already belonged to him. It had never not been his, but because he believed and lived the lie his evil Uncle Scar fed him, he forfeited the blessings over to the liar for a time. Simba's rejection of his rightful position had robbed his community of their blessings as well.

When we don't remember who we are in Christ, and whose we are, we live below the favor, blessings and daily gift of fresh mercies that belong to us, made available by the blood sacrifice of our risen Lord and Savior Jesus Christ. If we don't remember, and we choose to live with the lie satan "pins" on us when he pounces, we forfeit our inheritance over to him for a season just like Simba did. Because we are not positioned properly, our families, our communities and many others we know not of are also robbed of their blessings. Our actions or lack of action creates a ripple effect, even when we are unaware. Our choices matter.

But God, when in His richness—His faithfulness—His immeasurable love, pursues us, and we take initiative to hear from Him, we are reminded to remember! When we remember who we are and recall all He has done, fresh mercies freely flow and we are restored to our rightful position in Him once again. I remember a few years ago when the Lord pressed upon my mind to, *"Write the vision and make it plain on tablets, that he may run who reads it,"* just as he had instructed in *Habakkuk 2:2 NKJV.* I pondered these things in my heart but I'm recalling them now to my mind as I reflect on the faithfulness of my good Father who came to my rescue.

Like Jeremiah, I too will never forget that awful time when my grief overwhelmed me, though praise God, I was not consumed. Yet, I still dared to hope when I remembered: the unfailing love of the Lord never ends! He is a faithful God. He is my portion and He is enough for me. His mercies are fresh and new every morning and I will forever put my hope in Him!

At a moment when I was in deep sorrow, the Lord offered the gift of hope to my aching heart and drew me to His Word.

HURT IN THE WORLD
HEALED BY THE WOR

By Suzanne Grimaud

Just when I feared I'd forever stay stuck
in this never ending cycle of grief,
God restored me with hope, turned the grief for my good,
healed my mind and gave me relief.
He took the many hurts I'd gathered and held
from painful effects of sin in the world.
Then He healed my heart as He whispered the Truth
and delivered me from all fear through His Word.
I will never forget – I remember so well
all the Father has done for me.
He healed my marriage, my mind, my body, my dreams
and He rescued my family.
I know who I am and I know Whose I am.
I stand courageous with faith as my shield.
I will forever tell my story, giving God all the glory,
because I can, Good Grief—I'm Healed!

SECTION ONE

HURT IN THE WORLD

~

HEALED BY THE WORD!

CHAPTER 1

A HOLY WHISPER OF HOPE

He whispered a secret to me right in front of everyone standing there, but surprisingly no one else heard the sacred words my ears received. My heart was hurting. I was facing the hardest decision I would ever have to make in my marriage when the Holy Spirit spoke clearly to me in prayer that December night.

I heard these audible words after enjoying a holiday dinner in the home of friends, "Begin journaling your prayers and your quiet time with me, Suzanne. I will teach you and will reveal myself to you." Then as clear as day, He told me that my prayers had been heard and were responsible for saving my marriage. As we united in intercession, I was ushered into the most intimate presence of Jesus I had ever known. It was this vulnerable time in my life that I was in great need of comfort and direction when Jesus walked right into the room and spoke directly to my heart. I remember thinking I was being selfish to receive all the attention while our friends were standing there. These words and other intimate things Jesus spoke to me were so personal and I sensed His physical body stationed right in front of me, ignoring everyone else. I peaked my eyes open during prayer to verify my suspicions but did not see Him, however He was there in front of me, ministering to my grieving heart. I will never forget the beautiful encounter I had with the Lord that Christmas season of 2004.

My heart was freshly wounded and was physically hurting inside my chest. As a result, I was only trusting in Jesus and I clung to everything He told me in those moments. I bought my first prayer journal just days before His birthday in obedience to the voice of the Holy Spirit. It was His present to me that would provide for a deeper presence of Himself and a habit of entering into the secret place to receive my strength. He knew what lied ahead and that I was going to need a place to meet with Him and would need a space to create a record of requests and to archive answers received by faith. My faith would need an anchor point of reference as things were getting ready to get shaken up unbeknownst to me, and I would need "something" tangible to hold onto. Jesus was my "Someone" who would hold onto me, but He knew I would need a faith builder in my hand to remind me of His faithfulness, and I needed to start writing. His Spirit speaks directly to my heart but I've learned that He also speaks through my fingers when I grab a pen or a computer. It was His idea for me to begin journaling my time with Him and it has proven to provide a place of healing and intimate relationship I enjoy with my Savior still today.

My prayer for you as you begin to read my story (His story) is that no matter what your story is, you will receive the healing Word unto your soul, and that you and Jesus will make your story and His story in your life, history! Your history is behind you, but when His story is weaved in you, your history gets healed and made new, then it produces new stories of hope through you! I am compelled to reveal the reason for the hope I carry with the hopeful expectation you too will receive hope and healing for whatever your soul is depleted of. You may not feel you are in need of hope or healing and perhaps you are in a really good place with the Lord or you do not desire a relationship with Him. Wherever you find yourself right now, my hope is that you would be open to hearing me out because I'm telling you, when I felt like I was alone, destroyed and without hope…hope found me, and it's for you too.

A foundational disclaimer . . .

Before I expose the details throughout this book, of the hurt received in the world, I want to give God the glory as my story tells of transformation because He has used the pain to purify my heart and has given hope to countless others. I wonder if you, like I, have some similarities and have suffered the tragic untimely death of a close family member or have suffered the death of a dream or hopeful expectation. Maybe you have endured marriage difficulties or the destruction of it brought on by the effects of pornography or other sexual sins. You may have suffered much grief and pain in your life because of a number of reasons, and as a result, your mental health perhaps has been less than healthy. You may associate with the many who have had traumatic events served to them, or you may still be holding onto a grudge, offense, bitterness, or unforgiveness in your heart which is keeping you trapped in a cycle that leaves you feeling stuck. I was that hamster on the never-ending spinning wheel for twenty-five years but I am no longer captive in that cycle. I'm running freely on a path of wholeness and there is room for you too, my friend. Will you be willing to open up your heart and take a chance on yourself? Don't let the differences of our drama details deter you from diving in deeper and contending for your own personal path to healing. Let the life lessons I've learned lead you to press into the Lord as He reveals personal details to your own heart.

The Lord teaches us many things for purposes He has in mind to bring ultimate healing, restoration and hope! God takes all things and uses them for our good, His glory and to establish the Kingdom of Heaven through His children. As His beloved whom He loves and corrects, we must be willing to walk through a pruning / purifying fire in order to become a pure vessel God can fill so that when He pours Himself out of us into our communities - the impurities are not there. He is holy! We are to be holy as He is holy. It is His Holy Spirit in us that allows for us to be holy, but our vessels must be clean before His purpose in us may be carried out. When we willingly obey the promptings of the Holy Spirit's voice, we activate the purifying process in our hearts. In response, the Lord brings us into greater alignment with His will for our lives.

As we respond in faith with our action steps - God unlocks the next step so we may continue on our adventure walk with Jesus, one step at a time. The enemy sees us strolling the intimate path with our Savior, and gets worried because when God's children believe, pray, and move in faith, mountains are set in motion and he loses ground. So as a result, his fiery darts get lit up and released at the Father's sons and daughters. This is why the Word tells us to put on the FULL armor of God and take up the shield of faith daily, so that *when* the day of evil comes, we will stand.

Recognize the triggers . . .

Since we are aware the day of evil will come, it's important to know our weak spots, or rather our trigger points. You know the old saying, "Fool me once, shame on you. Fool me twice, shame on me." Well, when I reflect on the devil's schemes and attacks, I like to refer to the line from the movie, *"A Night at the Museum,"* and declare to the devil this: "Fool me once, shame on you. Fool me twice, shame on YOU." There is no shame or condemnation from God towards us; however, when we fall for the lies of the enemy and receive the shame he prompts, we pay the price. We need to reject the deceiver and shift the shame back to the source of it. We were not promised we would be pain free, but our pain allows the promises of God to work through us. If you can learn to recognize patterns, signs and triggers that have caused you to experience an episode of anxiety, fear or depression in the past, you can learn how to minimize or obliterate future episodes by changing your behavior, environment and by renewing your mind. I will share more on that later.

Suit up and get ready to take action . . .

Experience leaves clues, but we will still get blindsided if we are not paying attention. If we lower the shield, we give opportunity for attack. God himself places the helmet of salvation on our heads when we take hold of it. He places the breastplate of righteousness and the belt of truth on us when we ask Him to. He also gives the sword to us, which is His unparalleled, extremely sharp living and active Word. As we share the good news of the gospel of Christ, we receive the shoes

of peace on our feet, allowing us to walk with the Lord. But we must take up the shield of faith. We must pick it up and use it to activate the power faith carries with it. If we forget to hold it in place as we walk, fear comes after us. To take up the shield, we must put effort into action, which takes energy. However, if we get tired and weary, we become weak and may choose not to pick up and carry the shield of faith. This gives the devil the opportunity to hit the believer when least expected. We are usually not paying attention which is why we are suddenly surprised when we suffer setbacks. We can learn to evade the attacks if we realize that we may be vulnerable if not intentionally focusing our minds on putting the full armor on, and doing the things that we are aware of that will minimize trigger points.

Rest is essential . . .

It should not be surprising that we become targets of our spiritual enemy when we are worn out and depleted of rest. There were two specific times we are shown in the Word, that satan (little "s" on purpose) came at Jesus with an all out spiritual attack. Jesus was physically exhausted both times. The accounts that I'm referring to are of course, the desert temptations and then in the garden when Jesus was so weary and burdened because he was already carrying the weight of the sin of the world in preparation to put it to death on the cross. He surrendered His will to the will of the Father in the garden, then He literally sweat blood as He was in anguish because of His great love for us. Though Jesus triumphed through these evil trials, nonetheless, He still suffered and had to endure them in order to be able to complete the mission our Messiah came to do. His purpose was to defeat sin, destroy the works of the devil and save mankind. Jesus demonstrated by example that when we are at our weakest points and when we are exhausted, we are vulnerable, yet He is able to rescue us in the process.

Praise God we don't have to fulfill the mission Jesus completed but because we are His redeemed ones, we have become the targets of the enemy to inflict pain upon. He uses the same tactics he used on Jesus. It's never been about us, but if we are not careful, we will find ourselves wounded, inflicted and fearful because we forgot to use our powerful shield of faith weapon. Jesus' heart hurts when this happens because He loves us. He hurts when we hurt.

Now that you know, you know . . .

Knowledge brings responsibility with it and when we gain wisdom and knowledge of how we become spiritually weak and tired, it is our personal responsibility to guard against it. We are all different and due to our personality, culture, experience and physical as well as spiritual maturity, our tiresome trigger points may vary. We must remain aware and alert, with full armor on, then standing up we must firmly stand!

The Word of God is our firm foundation we stand on and because I have found so much personal healing through the applied Word of God in my life, my faith is strong and unshakeable. I will share many scriptures with you throughout the remaining chapters of this treasured true tale that have been a key to my mental healing. If you have a Bible, you may want to look these passages up for yourself if they resonate with you. You may wish to download a digital Bible to use, but there is nothing like holding the written Word in your hands, underlining verses that are meaningful to your heart and mind, and recording special moments in the back or along the edges. It will surely become a personal treasure and an heirloom for your children, their children and their children's children. You may want to write down some of the verses I share in your own prayer journal as well as truths the Holy Spirit highlights to you. It will be good to refer back to your journal at times when you need a faith builder or when you want to go and see all the Lord has done since you penned the promises in His presence. You will be amazed at answers to prayer and you will also be encouraged to see how you are growing in the faith over time. Dare to try it.

As I read it, write it, declare it, believe it, and live it out, the Word of God (Sword) comes alive to me and in me. The Holy Spirit guides us into all truth and will even use the inspired Bible to speak to your heart. I cannot effectively communicate my story without including prayers and passages from the Word alongside my journey because they go together like peanut butter and jelly. The Lord continues His healing work in my heart and mind as I seek Jesus, remain in a relationship with Him, listen for His voice, speak and do what I hear the Holy Spirit say and do, and as I believe in His promises and I trust in Christ alone. I hope you will be inspired to journey deeper with the Lord because God will ultimately use your intentional effort to alter your future and align your mind with the mind of Christ. He will whisper holy words of hope to your searching soul and will bring healing to your mind, to your heart and to your bones.

Put On the Full Armor of God (Ephesians 6:10-18 NIV)

Finally, be strong in the Lord and in his mighty power. Put on the full armor of God, so that you can take your stand against the devil's schemes. For our struggle is not against flesh and blood, but against the rulers, against the authorities, against the powers of this dark world and against the spiritual forces of evil in the heavenly realms. Therefore put on the full armor of God, so that when the day of evil comes, you may be able to stand your ground, and after you have done everything, to stand. Stand firm then, with the belt of truth buckled around your waist, with the breastplate of righteousness in place, and with your feet fitted with the readiness that comes from the gospel of peace. In addition to all this, take up the shield of faith, with which you can extinguish all the flaming arrows of the evil one. Take the helmet of salvation and the sword of the Spirit, which is the word of God. And pray in the Spirit on all occasions with all kinds of prayers and requests. With this in mind, be alert and always keep on praying for all the Lord's people.

Your history is behind you, but when His story is weaved in you, your history gets healed and made new, then it produces new stories of hope through you!

CHAPTER 2

BRIGHT LIGHT
EXPOSES DARKNESS

After the anguish of a few unforeseen episodes, I recognize familiar signs that led me down a path to a mental imbalance and a physical crash, then ultimately to an all out attack on my spirit. Each time I've endured the event, I've gained new wisdom and have processed through it with the healing Word applied as a weapon. As I've paid attention to the pattern, I thought I had figured out how to self-preserve and prevent further attacks. It wasn't until this fourth blow, early in 2020, that the Lord gave me insight as to why periodically I have experienced painful mental messes, and with this new knowledge, I am hopeful. I am not excited to have gone through these frightening experiences, which I will share with you later, but I fully believe God wants to use them for His glory.

Though the trials have been something I never desire to repeat, I am grateful for the outcome of wholeness and for the heightened dependency on and relationship I have with the Lord because of it. I

it is wise to pursue an intimate friendship and reliance on Je-
id never quit seeking to be in His presence. Then when you go through a spiritual battle, you will be able to stand and let the Lord fight for you and bring you safely through it. This is the part of my testimony I've never wanted to publish in word or in writing but the Lord has made it clear I am to disclose and expose the enemy's tactics. I'm turning the narrative and flipping on the floodlight, which always breaks the darkness.

The journey turns scary if out of nowhere an enemy's fiery dart hits your back when your shield has been down. My aim is to keep the shield held high by not becoming tired and weary. I must give my body rest, and I must remain in His rest. This is how we stay "shield in place" ready. The Holy Spirit is teaching me, as I trust Him to do so. The victory is His!

Another way to keep our shields in place is that the body of Christ needs to unify in purpose and be authentic with each other so we can be a "watchman on the wall" for each other. In other words, we need to alert our brothers and sisters in Christ of how we have discerned a spiritual attack so we can help cover each other in prayer and help to prevent an invasion in someone else's life. Knowledge is key to averting trials. The devil may be sneaky, but we the people of God have an advantage because we have the authority and power over the enemy and when we team up in groups of two or three, he is powerless over us. That is a promise of God. A lifestyle of repentance and dependence is perhaps the best spiritual insurance policy we can hold. When the Holy Spirit speaks of how you may have let someone offend you, repent of it quickly. Be truthful with how you are feeling and share it (confess it) with someone. Pray and ask the Lord to heal the wounds and to give you an opportunity to make it right if you are to speak about it further. Forgive freely. Then, when you have that "stirring in your spirit" to speak up in order to give clarity or to confront in love, do not delay so a bitter root does not grow.

As a personal example, at an event recently, I was saddened and grieved by a private situation. I shared my heart with someone close who later alluded to it in front of others and without realizing, spoke a word that brought confusion to a dear friend. Later, in the night in the middle of my sleep, the Holy Spirit quickened me to pray. My friend texted me the next morning because the Holy Spirit woke her up and prompted her to start a conversation about the confusion that she was suddenly made aware of when she awakened. As it turns out, there had been a communication misunderstanding that was easily cleared up. The resolve was painless because we both chose to listen to the promptings of the Holy Spirit and we prayed and we addressed it instead of dwelling on what we thought about what had happened.

The result in the end was that love won. God won. We won. The devil's tactics to destroy a friendship or insert bitterness failed. He had taken advantage of a communication misunderstanding to aim a fiery dart at the hearts of two women, but we were both alerted by the Holy Spirit dwelling in us, and by faith, we acted on it with full armor on, and extinguished the flames of the arrows. That is a testimony worth sharing of how wearing the full armor of God allows us to stand. If we had instead let bitterness take root in our hearts by ignoring the conversation and burying the emotion, the root would have grown and perhaps caused a division in our friendship and in the ministry we do together. It doesn't take much to get us off course of our walk of purity and power, and if we get off course just a little, before long, we are way off the path. It is then that we are vulnerable to another problem because the battle is in the mind. The mind is where we dwell over what is good or what is bothering us. It is this place that we must guard so we will remain in a place of safety, under the protective feathers of our almighty God. He keeps in perfect peace those who keep their minds stayed on Him.

Whose plan are you following? . . .

There have been a few times I've received a word of direction from the Lord and sometimes even a detailed plan, then in my excitement, I find myself moving quickly and trying to put my own ideas to flight and will sometimes get things out of His order. I'm sure this does not happen to you, but I will often take on too much or go beyond what the Lord told me to do. I guess I think that when He gives an idea, it's up to me to run with it without consulting Him as I expand on His original command, like I can make it better. Uh…Right! The result is, I take over and change the plans to be my plans that are quickly rolling. I have at this time faded the line and I don't even notice what I've done. Now, I'm perhaps carrying a heavy load the Lord never asked me or intended for me to carry, but my clouded vision assumes that I am in step with Him. I am on the right path, but the pace is off and I find I'm out of His rest. I guess when He says, *"Be still, and know that I am God,"* He means it. The Lord communicates to us when we need to hear not only the "yes, go this way" directives, but also the words "no, be still and wait."

The wounded warrior…

When our "out of His rest" journey also includes intercessory prayer, fatigue intersects the physical body with emotions, which are usually heightened in the spiritual realm where we've been doing battle in prayer. It is this place of vulnerability that presents an opportunity for a fiery dart to be shot at the prayer warrior who is exhausted and the weakened intercessor receives the wounding.

This is exactly what happened to me just days after completing the mission of driving around the state of Oklahoma in intercessory prayer with a few friends early in 2020 as the Lord directed and guided us. It was a beautiful encounter I will never forget. We sang as we worshipped the Lord, prayed and prophetically staked tent pegs into the four corners of the state asking the Lord to purify, cleanse and heal our land. In essence, we were securing the borders of our state in the heavenly realm as we traveled, prayed and depended on God to give instruction. We prayed with and for people everywhere we stopped and we blessed them as we let them know we were completing a prayer drive around the state to seek the Lord's favor on Oklahoma. We went with the Governor's knowledge and blessing and with teams of prayer partners journeying with us through intercessory prayer coverage.

Our traveling tribe of four repented on behalf of different people groups and native tribes we were identifying with in prayer and we asked the Lord's blessings and resources to fall upon Oklahoma. We also asked the Lord to use Oklahoma as a launching pad to turn the hearts of our nation back to God. We prayed for forgiveness, racial and tribal reconciliation, protection, healing, marriages and families to be restored, natural resources to come forth, financial wealth, and for the supernatural hand of God to deliver our state from evil as Oklahoma repents and turns back to God. In faith we still believe for this to happen! We stood in the gap for many who have been deceived, have been abandoned, rejected, or have suffered soul wounding, trauma, pain or poverty. The Lord would give us signs, clues or thoughts that would inspire what we were to cover next. We experienced a heaven hosted prayer scavenger hunt as we literally followed the leading of the Holy Spirit. It was light, easy and fun!

I am grateful I was able to participate and that God provided a way for me to be obedient to what He had birthed in my prayer partner and myself a year earlier. The only thing is that before the journey began, due to many circumstances beyond my control and some that I unknowingly created, my body was exhausted. My shield was down at the onset of the prayer drive and as a result, extreme fatigue set in, both physically and spiritually. A few days after our return, my husband went on a trip and while he was away, my tired body and mind took a dive. Fear found an opportunity to creep in then I got hit hard physically with an anxiety attack in the middle of the night and with a three week spiritual battle in my mind. The higher we climb, the lower we fall should we suffer a physiological crash. It had been three weeks of exhaustion building up when my body literally shut down, so it's no wonder it was a three-week recovery.

By the grace of God and the wisdom given me through Godly men and women, I now have a greater understanding of how my physical and spiritual attack was made possible. This was the fourth time, all occurring since January 2005 and I believe that it was the last time because of what the Lord has since revealed to me, purified in me and because of what He is doing through me now. My desire is to expose the enemy's tactics and give healing strategy to the weary. Reader… read to the end! The devil aimed at my mind, my family, my marriage and the ministry God prepared for me. He set out to destroy what God had created. He thought he would get away with it but the enemy overplayed his hand because the truth of God's Word tells me in

1 John 4:4b NASB, "…greater is He who is in you than he who is in the world."

Don't play with that fire . . .

Someone wise recently spoke this divine word gift from the Holy Spirit to me. As I was receiving counsel from Rev. Jay Jellison, with Becoming Love Ministries, he spoke a nugget of truth that enlightened my soul. He said, "If you are a recovering alcoholic, it would be a bad idea for you to go into a bar thinking you could easily avoid a drink which in turn would cause you to be in bondage again if you partook of it. The same goes for you, Suzanne. Because you have learned that when you are physically exhausted and emotionally charged, and then you enter into deep spiritual intercessory prayer, you give opportunity for your body to crash. Once that happens, the opportunity for the enemy to hit you while your body is weak has been made possible. It is like thinking you can play with fire but not get burned."

The good news is this scenario does not have to be presented again because I have been given insight from the Holy Spirit how to be prepared and positioned to stand with my full armor on, my shield and sword held up, and with confident hope in place. I now take rest and mindfulness seriously and have let several responsibilities go. The Lord is a gentle teacher and I'm grateful for the wakeup call.

Armor On ~ Shields Up! . . .

The shield of faith and the sword of the spirit are the two weapons we carry in our hands that ensure our victory. In the Book of Revelation, we read that when we endure to the end, we win the prize of salvation and eternity in heaven. It says in *Revelation 12:11 NKJV, "…they overcame him, by the blood of the Lamb and by the word of their testimony…"* The blood of the Lamb is of course the price Jesus paid with His life on the cross. He has already won the victory by His resurrection. Our belief in the truth of God's Word, the sword of the spirit allows our victory weapon to defeat the devil's attacks and schemes. The Word of God destroys the plans of the enemy!

Remember, another way we are victorious overcomers is by using the faith shield (our defensive and offensive weapon). The offense moves toward the enemy. Faith walks and takes action! That is how our faith is activated and defeats fear. So even when we have allowed a dart to hit us with our shield down, we can pick it back up and start moving forward. Faith in God always defeats fear that comes against us. We can realize the presence of fear without receiving the present of fear. Fear is an unwanted gift from satan that we have to accept in order to be inflicted by it, though we may still be affected by it even when we reject it. It is a weapon forged against us but the Lord says that no weapon formed against us shall prosper. We do not have to take it. In fact, we must not even entertain the thought of it. That is why it's critical that we realize we are overcomers by the Word of our testimony as the book of Revelation reveals.

When we open up our mouths and speak, we declare a thing! We verbalize in agreement with what we believe and in whom we believe in. So if we find ourselves under attack, we must activate our sword and speak the truth of God's Word and we must make known our testimony of what we believe in faith to be true. *"Faith shows the reality of what we hope for; it is the evidence of things we cannot see." Hebrews 11:1 NLT* We know by faith in the Word that the unseen realm is the real and eternal life. What is seen now is temporary. As children of God, our bodies can be inflicted, harmed or killed, but our real eternal spiritual self cannot because we are safe in the arms of God. When we abide in this truth and declare with our mouths of our glorious hope, trust and faith in our unseen God, the victorious rescue mission is activated. Why? Because faith activates and to keep a stable mind, we must activate our faith filled minds.

Our faith shields literally extinguish the fiery darts coming at us. They fall to the ground as we walk by faith. It is then, that we can stand. We take the territory as we move forward in faith, and then we are able to hold our position and watch the enemy flee. The Bible tells us to resist the devil and he will flee from you. The opposite is true as well. If we do not resist but instead agree with his sneaky lies, he will not flee but will set up camp. His camp includes fear, anxiety, confusion, depression, and a playground set up in your mind to bring tormenting lies. Do not agree with the devil. Resist him as you rest in the promises of God and move in faith believing that your unseen God is fighting your battles for you. Remain calm and cast your cares upon the Lord for He cares for you. He has already won the victory. Believe it!

All of this is absolutely true and I can and do give testimony to the healing power in my life through the Word of God and my faith testimony coming together. No one can tell me differently because I have miraculously been pulled through mental physical crashes in rapid time because the Holy Spirit in me has taught me how to return to rest. I've left this part of my testimony out for years but I am realizing it is this part that so many need to hear, so I will get real and let you in on what I've faced in order to build your faith and give God the glory in the midst of my healing story.

Faith in God always defeats fear that comes against us. We can realize the presence of fear without receiving the present of fear.

CHAPTER 3

FIGHT, FLIGHT, FREEZE
OR FRIGHT

"Fight, flight or freeze" sounds like a game children play on the school playground which is ironic because it is actually a game our bodies play in response to the game played on the playground of the mind when it anticipates fear (fright) or danger. As I've already admitted, I see that at times I have participated in either allowing my body to be physically exhausted or my emotions to be supercharged when called into spiritual warfare. The combination has led to a physiological response accompanied by an extreme anxiety driven panic attack and a flood of sudden irrational fears. The body responds to imminent perceived danger by preparing it for fight or flight. The body begins to prepare itself to fight infections, shut down certain functions and store up what's needed for what it perceives to be short of. This is the fight scenario. If the body goes into flight mode, it will literally go AWOL and run away or shut down. It may also go into a temporary freeze mode while trying to anticipate what to do next. If this happens, you are at the mercy of your compromised command center to act on your behalf, and it is not always the desired destination you are taken to. The best way to avoid this hostile takeover is to be prepared ahead of time, and that is what I mostly want to share with you in this book. I believe the Lord is teaching me how to keep physical and emotional balance and rest in Him so that when called upon for intercession or for an assignment, I will be prepared as an arrow in the Master's hand, not as a target for the enemy. God is leading and teaching me, as I trust Him. My prayer is that He will continue to refine me and restore me in the process, and that I can impart to you what I have gained through experience and by leaning on the help of the Holy Spirit.

We know that satan can represent himself as an angel of light. But as a child of the King of kings who is my Good Shepherd, I know and hear His voice. We are to test the spirits. I also believe there are times it is necessary to call upon others to carry the shield with you and watch and pray for you. We are not to go alone but to involve our "tribe" as a cord of three strands is not easily broken. God gives the body of Christ to each other to cover, protect, encourage and strengthen. Then when we are done and in need of rest, someone must hold the shield over us and for us, until we are able to stand again. Even while we sleep, after we have engaged in frontline work through intercessory prayer, we need others to cover us in prayer as we replenish what we have poured out. It's a way of protecting the seed that was sown.

Watchmen have your back . . .

We are not to be "Lone Rangers" in ministry because when we are, we become easy prey and can be easily picked off. As a personal watchman for my spiritual family, the Body of Christ, which includes you, I am compelled to share from my experience how to keep our armor on and our guards up so the sneaky one cannot attack any of us. We need each other so it's necessary to put aside our differences, stand shoulder to shoulder with each other and we must blow the enemy's cover! We must be unified in the Spirit and working together so we can operate as one Body of Christ, staying alert and walking in the authority Jesus has given us. When we have been victorious over fear or sin in a particular area, we have greater authority in that same arena to help others to be overcomers as well. Our testimony is powerful!

Speak up and find you're not alone . . .

When we allow our bodies to get out of balance and fatigued, we permit a physiological setup for a mental breakdown to occur. We must take care of our bodies and our minds just like we have to take care of our hearts. I am grateful that God has given me insight, grace and tools to assist others as we heal and return to balance. It is tempting to think, "I am alone in this and that surely no one else has experienced the things I have. Who could possibly understand what I thought, witnessed, feared and experienced?" I know this is not true as the Word says not to be surprised at the fiery trials you are going through, as if something strange were happening to you. The devil knows if he can keep us quiet, then the children of God who are free in Christ, will believe they are not free and will remain held in the bondage of fear. But as we confess our sins to one another, and pray for one another, we are healed. This truth spoken unlocks not only healing for ourselves through our testimony, but it also gives others permission to share their own personal experiences and receive their healing too. Faith trumps fear! Mercy triumphs over judgment, and freedom is released to us when we realize it was already made available for us by the blood of Jesus that was shed on the cross. Whom the son sets free is truly free indeed.

Pruned and purified . . .

Be mindful that when you are made aware that the Lord is asking you to activate your faith in a new way, you may also receive a new level of pruning and purifying. He may reveal things He desires to clean in you so He can freely work through you. It may cause pain but He never wastes your pain. God's plans are for you, not against you. Trust Him as He heals deep wounds, past trauma, painful memories and wrong belief systems you've created and lived by because of your experience. As you partner with the Lord and allow Him to pull up harmful weeds by the root, He replaces them with healthy roots of the fruit of His Spirit and He will gently teach you His ways.

Trust His process and allow His work to begin to work in your life and bring new life to you. That is real freedom and I am just beginning to realize it. *Romans 8:14 NLT says, "For all who are led by the Spirit of God are children of God."* It's that child-like faith and innocence of heart that our Father wants to see in us as we walk in relationship with Him and as we live by the power of the Holy Spirit within us doing through us what only He can do. That is how we live the free life. If you are not free and would like to experience this abundant life, pause now and ask Jesus into your heart. Tell Him you believe in Him and believe He died for your sins, was raised to life and is able to raise you to new life too. He wants to be your Savior, your healer, and in relationship with you as your friend. If you are not ready, tell Jesus all about what you are thinking and feeling and ask Him to open up your mind and heart as you continue to read. It is a step of faith but He will meet you right where you are and by His Spirit, He will walk the next step with you. Receive Jesus if you will and be filled with the gift of His Holy Spirit.

My mind was set . . .

Before I describe a few experiences I've had at times while briefly out of mental balance, I want to be clear about something. Even though my body has suffered a physiological attack due to exhaustion, high levels of cortisol, buildup of serotonin in my brain and gut, and an emotional overload, my mind and my soul have always been at peace. This is not the same peace the world knows of but rather the peace the Holy Spirit produces in the Spirit-filled life.

Though my thoughts were out of control because of my brain receiving transmissions during a crisis moment, my mind "stayed" on Christ and He kept me at perfect peace. Peace in the storm, joy in the chaos and revelation in the middle of turmoil are gifts from the Spirit. There may have been a storm raging in my mind at times, but I have not drowned or been overtaken by the high waves. My eyes always lock on Jesus and on the truth of God's Word. I truly dwell in the presence of the Almighty and I rest in the shadows of the Most High

God and when I am in trouble, I take shelter in the arms of the Lord. He is my ever-present help in times of need.

> *"This is why the Scriptures say: Things never discovered or heard of before, things beyond our ability to imagine— these are the many things God has in store for all his lovers. But God now unveils these profound realities to us by the Spirit. Yes, he has revealed to us his inmost heart and deepest mysteries through the Holy Spirit, who constantly explores all things. After all, who can really see into a person's heart and know his hidden impulses except for that person's spirit? So it is with God. His thoughts and secrets are only fully understood by his Spirit, the Spirit of God. For we did not receive the spirit of this world system but the Spirit of God, so that we might come to understand and experience all that grace has lavished upon us. And we articulate these realities with the words imparted to us by the Spirit and not with the words taught by human wisdom. We join together Spirit-revealed truths with Spirit-revealed words. Someone living on an entirely human level rejects the revelations of God's Spirit, for they make no sense to him. He can't understand the revelations of the Spirit because they are only discovered by the illumination of the Spirit. Those who live in the Spirit are able to carefully evaluate all things, and they are subject to the scrutiny of no one but God. For who has ever intimately known the mind of the Lord Yahweh well enough to become his counselor? Christ has, and we possess Christ's perceptions."* 1 Corinthians 2:9-16 TPT

Out of balance . . .

When I crashed this last time, due to a chemical imbalance going on in my brain, I became confused and had trouble sleeping at night. I felt overwhelmed and because the clock was ticking while my thoughts were settling down, there were a few weeks I incorrectly "connected dots" in my head. I began to fear again but would face each lie the enemy tried to get me to agree with, by activating my faith. It was a process I had to encounter head-on. Inside my mind, I did not trust some of the people I love the most because I perceived things incorrectly. Personal motives can be pure and right but still be used by the enemy to incorrectly confirm a lie he presents to someone who is not balanced physiologically. What I mean is that when a body is out of balance mentally, an opportunity has been created for satan to take advantage of and twist truths to bring further confusion.

In the garden, he said to Eve, *"Did God really say not to eat the fruit from the trees of the garden?"* He took a little truth and twisted it to present a lie that would bring doubt, confusion and a conversation that would lead to sin. The sin of not believing and trusting God is all it takes to bring destruction to another level. Satan does not create. He is not creative. He only comes to kill, steal and destroy. He takes a good thing, a truth if you will, a promise of God, and he packages it so you will stop and ponder the new possibilities he is presenting to you in the form of a lie. When we let our minds ponder, or wonder, we have stepped into a setup for a distraction of what is holy and true, and it becomes our downfall.

We are told in the Word of God to put on the full armor of God so we may be able to stand against the devil's schemes. According to Oxford Languages online dictionary, the definition of schemes is *a large-scale systematic plan or arrangement for attaining some particular object or putting an idea into effect. To make plans, especially in a devious way or with intent to do something illegal or wrong, to conspire, plot, connive or maneuver your plan with intent to bring harm.* Don't be deceived. Schemes are evil but are powerless against the armored children of God.

Twisted words fuel fear; Peace of God frees from all fear . . .

The devil's schemes and plans to harm us are indeed tricky. He waits for moments when we have either foolishly let our guard down or we are physically weak. But when we have our armor on, we have our mind stayed on Christ. Even in our weakness, He is strong in us. As we carry the Holy Spirit in our heart, when a fiery dart hits us in the back, the Holy Spirit sustains us and gives us peace. The peace that comes from God, as a gift of the Holy Spirit is the peace we all long for but it's only a place of rest to those who have received the Holy

Spirit as a deposit from Jesus. We walk in it often without
but when in a moment of crisis, peace that passes all und
truly does guard the heart in mind of all who are in Christ Jesus.
spoke peace and the storm became still. He still calms the storms as
we release His peace all around us. We are able to do that when we are
abiding in a place of rest in Him. We must remain in His presence to
remain in His peace.

Recently, I had a vision of an eye of the Lord. With my eyes
closed, I saw one beautiful open eye of Jesus, complete with long soft
eyelashes. The iris was in the shape of a bomb burst star and it was
fiery bronze in color. I saw a dove flying back and forth in the eye
and it was colored in the hues of the rainbow. The eye was full of
compassion and love as He gazed at me. As I processed the vision, I
asked the Lord to tell me what He was showing me. The Holy Spirit
spoke to my spirit and I heard this: Suzanne, My peace is not only
not like the peace the world gives, but it is also not delivered the same
way the world receives peace. My peace guards your heart and mind
as you remain in Me. The eye is the window of the soul and your soul
is guarded by My peace. My peace is a promise. The Holy Spirit is a
promise I have put in you as you dwell in Me. Keep your eyes locked
on My eyes, and as you do, I will transfer My love to you. Because I
dwell in you, your eyes become My eyes when you are fixing your eyes
on Mine. Then, when you lock eyes with the ones I put in front of you,
and you show My love to them, I will make a deposit of my Father's
love to them through your eyes of love. They will be drawn to Me!
You will be able to share the Good News of the gospel with them. My
peace I leave you and my peace I give to you, "not as the world gives" so
do not let your hearts be troubled and do not be afraid." Wow! I didn't
expect that beautiful picture or personal message when I went to bed,
or when I suddenly woke up, but my spirit was rested and listening
and the Word of God spoke to my spirit. I have confident hope and
assurance of the evidence of what is unseen.

I've shared this vision with several and I am hearing back how the
Lord has been reminding them to look people in the eyes. His love
is being poured out to strangers in diners, in grocery stores and everywhere we go. Look at people with the love of God and talk to them.

That is not normal in our world but is the normal Christian life in the Kingdom of God. Look upon the Lord. He is beautiful and is worthy of sharing with the people of this world who desperately need to know Him. Lock your eyes on Jesus. Receive His love. Let His peace guard your heart and mind and accept the promise of the Holy Spirit to dwell in your life. Your eyes will become His eyes and His love will flow through your eyes and transfer His peace to the ones in front of you. It is this peace that helps my mind be at peace even when my body is out of balance. It has the power to transform me as I renew my mind. I'm grateful for the beautiful word picture the Lord dropped into my spirit. It was a gift and I treasure it.

Citizens of Heaven living on earth . . .

We who belong to Christ still live in this world and are affected by it and by the sin that is operating in it. However, as citizens of heaven, we are not of this world though we are in it, and we are not obligated to embrace or receive personally the effects that sin brings along with it. As we are dealing with a historic worldwide virus from China, I have become aware that though it appears we are fighting with flesh and blood, the real enemy of our souls was behind this terrible plague. The virus is awful and real, of course, but the real plague that was unleashed is fear, which has proven more deadly than the virus itself. I'm not talking about fear of getting the virus, as there is always a healthy fear that produces actions of wisdom. I want to be careful with my words because I do not want to be misunderstood.

The undercurrent of fear that has been unleashed goes way deeper than the obvious surface issues many, including myself, have experienced conflict over. I'm calling it out because I wish to live in harmony and unity with my brothers and sisters in Christ and not allow the enemy to plant new roots of offense and bitterness in my heart. Relationships are more important than disagreements and when we recognize "who" started the conflict, we can band together in perfect love and cast out all fear.

Fear is of the devil and he is a liar. Many have embraced the fear gift and have agreed with the lie that we are never going to be well again. I saw a post going around FaceBook recently I was troubled by. This was the caption on the meme: "Embrace the Suck!" I looked it up on Google, and this is what I found as the meaning: The situation is bad, but deal with it. It is referring to a messed up place crawling with bad guys. It is a military slang phrase coined in the Middle East during war. The message is: You can't change it so suck it up and deal with it, or embrace it. The post was referring to our current situation concerning how we are to operate, respond and embrace the bad that was going on around us and cannot be changed. We've had a virus, isolation, and supply shortage, lack of personal contact, murder, riots, human trafficking exposure, election fraud and extreme levels of anxiety all around the globe. It has been a rough year, I admit, but choosing to "embrace the suck" produces a victim and prisoner mentality. If I were to choose to embrace such a thing, I would be holding dear to the "lie gift" the enemy handed me. No thank you! I will not embrace it! I will reject the suck!

Our faith shields are not activated when we allow the twisted words of our adversary to be embraced. But there is hope! You CAN take your words back. You can receive revelation from the Holy Spirit, and you can turn towards the HOPE that lies before you. There is joy and freedom when we embrace the truth instead of the suck. We have authority over all the powers of darkness, and over rulers and principalities of this dark world. Jesus said it and I believe it! Let's unite as the Body of Christ and embrace our inheritance as co-heirs of Christ. Let's speak to the suck and snuff out its oxygen. Let's put fear to death by feeding our faith. We feed our faith when we feast upon the Word of God. Let's embrace our faith and start walking in it as we abide in the shadow and rest of the Almighty.

Is it legal? . . .

We are legal citizens of heaven the moment we receive the gift of salvation. When we receive by faith the gift of the Holy Spirit, our eyes are open to realize our citizenship has transitioned to an eternity in the Kingdom of God. Our legal identity is in Jesus Christ. So when the enemy plots schemes against us, he is asking our permission to give him legal authority to carry out his plans for our lives. He cannot take authority from you, but by your agreement with your mouth and actions, you might inadvertently give him authority to deceive you. Our words carry the ability to bless or to curse. Our words, or rather our testimony gives us the ability to overcome him or to be overcome by him. Remember our verse in *Revelation 12:11, "and they overcame him by the blood of the lamb, and by the word of their testimony…"*

A testimony is a written or spoken statement or word, especially one given in a court of law. It is used as evidence or proof provided by the existence or appearance of something. It, the word, serves as a witness, verification, confirmation or manifestation. A word makes things legal and binding. If your word that proceeds from your mouth is the Word of God or is your words of agreement and belief in Jesus, then you are under the legal authority of Heaven, in the highest courts of Heaven, where Jesus sits as King, ruler, judge and your defender.

However, if your word testimony agrees with lies and if you walk by fear instead of faith, you give authority over to the enemy to legally carry out his games. He has at this point stolen your faith and confident assurance as the child of God you are. Do not be dismayed or afraid! Again, there is hope! You are not doomed or left in that place. Repent, turn back the other way and receive healing by choosing to pick up the shield of faith again. Speak the promises of God out loud. Saturate in the Word and remind your soul to praise the Lord. When you speak in agreement with who God created you to be and you speak the opposite of the lies by speaking the truth of God's word, your mouth makes your ears hear and you activate your faith. Peace is released and the presence of God protects you from eternal harm.

Our bodies are temporary but our souls are eternal. *Revelation 12:11* says, *"They overcame…and they did not love their lives so much as to shrink from death."* We are spiritual beings living in a temporary body. Overcomers are safely sheltered in the arms of God. Declare that promise and walk confidently by faith, which is your shield. And if you drop your shield, pick it up again. When arrows have hit me through anxiety attacks, brain imbalances and physical breakdowns in my body, though I have always maintained internal and external peace of mind, I have also experienced symptoms that have been hard for me to mention.

I lost my balance . . .

Admittedly, while in the middle of a traumatic episode, I have feared "admission of these things" would end in an admission into a place that I did not want to go and did not belong. My ability to remain calm and prevent a situation I did not want has come only because of my reliance on the Holy Spirit to keep me at perfect peace. I have also been able to recognize that my thinking was not quite right and I have intentionally chosen to trust God to help me by trusting he's working through the people I love. Because of a chemical imbalance in the brain, what is perceived to be fact is not necessarily true. And because the enemy is working hard to trip me, he validates real facts known to me and to others all around me, to feed and confirm the lies he's spoken to me. This pattern creates a battle in my mind that I must fight. Realize this: The battle is always fought in the mind! The weapons used against me have always shown up in the form of past fears I have had in my life. The fear "dot" is then improperly connected in my brain to a fact "dot" and a lie is unleashed.

The schemes have included innocent situations and well-meaning, good people that are unaware their behaviors and words have been twisted in my mind and have produced an irrational fear. Some of these thoughts are subtle and simple but others have been sensational and systematic which caused my mind to fear a large-scale plan will certainly be carried out. These plans that I fear, if carried out, will come against not only myself but the ones I love as well as the entire body of Christ, so my mind has told me. As a daughter of God, with my mind set on Christ, trusting in Jesus, as I allow the healing to come, I've learned to trust my family to help me receive and take medications that assist in the process. The end goal when we begin is to wean off the meds when they have done their job and it is safe to do so. Another fear in taking medications has tried to grip me suggesting I would become addicted to the drugs and become foggy minded forever with prolonged use.

I have again been intentional in my prayers as I put my trust in God and have activated my faith by cooperating peacefully with the process. It has pained me to allow my family to know that I don't trust them at times but again, a chemical imbalance literally causes "dots"

orrectly connected in the brain and the emotions will often
y your secret irrational and temporary beliefs. My heart hurts
y fears hurt their hearts. I am thankful for the grace-filled,
loving and understanding family and friends who have walked this
journey to wholeness with me. I know what I've experienced in my
own mind but I cannot fathom what they have experienced in theirs
as they have been blindsided each time my body has without notice
crashed and I have behaved in a way that does not line up with who I
am. I know it has caused trauma to my loved ones as well. Praise God
He brings healing to our souls when truth enters the trauma. There
are treasures in our trauma when the Lord comes to our rescue. Truth
triumphs over trauma! Here is a morsel of truth found in *Proverbs
3:25 NIV "Have no fear of sudden disasters or of the ruin that overtakes the
wicked."* Remember this Word as you stand, *"For God has not given us
a spirit of fear, but of power and of love and of a sound mind." 2 Timothy
1:7 NKJV*

*Let's put fear to death by feeding our faith. We feed our faith
when we feast upon the Word of God.*

CHAPTER 4

RAW AND REAL

When under a physical or spiritual attack, the senses are heightened. I do not know if this is a symptom others have experienced, but again, I am just getting real with you as to what I have gone through in hopes to help you know there is hope and that if you can relate, you are not alone or weird.   During a brain imbalance, I become very aware of sounds, rhythms, undertones and every word I hear. I do not process them as I do when in balance. I have also audibly heard the lies of the enemy at times. It is scary to me when that has happened but I have also been aware that I do not have to believe what I hear. I then have to sort out the truth from the lies as well as the truth that just got twisted in my mind because of a chemical imbalance. I require quiet so I can sort through what I've heard, then focus on God's Word and on what I know to be true, noble, lovely, admirable, excellent and praiseworthy.

We are told to be transformed by the renewing of our mind and the way we renew our mind is by what we choose to dwell and think upon. When we have a battle going on in our mind, it is vitally important that we apply the Word of God to each thought that presents itself against the knowledge of God. We are to take each thought captive and make it obedient to Christ. We do that with the Word of God. To silence the lies, the chatter must cease because I am aware that it is being used against me when I am not well. I have to turn the noise of the radio, TV, Internet, social media, and telephone off, and I have to limit the talking to a minimum.

It is hard for others to understand as they can listen to the same sounds and see what I see yet not hear what I hear or perceive what I see. Loud noises at this time also literally hurt my head. I can feel the throbbing and the rhythm of the beats of every sound. Even water sounds like music and carries a beat with it that causes me to count or march to the rhythm. It makes my mind feel like I cannot turn it off and so entering into rest is difficult. Jesus said if we don't praise Him, the rocks will cry out. That makes total sense to me now as during these mental meltdowns, I hear sounds in everything! Perhaps everything truly is already praising the Lord but we don't hear it with our earthly ears. One day, when everything is restored, we will be aware and will harmonize our praise of our King along with all of creation. But until then, when mentally out of balance, this awareness makes it hard to focus; however, the Lord has taught me ways to shut it down. I will share tools and tips in a later chapter that are practical and useful and will hopefully help you as well.

The body was created by God to function perfectly but because sin is in the world, the curse brought an interruption to God's design. Because of Jesus, we are able to live abundant lives in spite of our decaying bodies. I don't understand why some people die early like my mother and baby sister did. I don't understand why some people live with disease, pain or other body issues while others receive healing on this earth. I do understand we have hope for a perfectly healed and resurrected body that will be transformed into the likeness of Jesus and will last an eternity. I know that I know that God is working even when I don't see it and that is the place that my faith is activated. If you are suited up in your battle gear before a battle begins, you will be able to stand once the battle is over. The beautiful truth that helps me fight the battles I face is that I am aware the battle belongs to the

Lord. I am to remain calm! Victory is His!

Soldier Mentality . . .

As we surrender our heart, will and plan to the Lord, abiding in His Word and responding to the Holy Spirit, we will be able to hold our position. On our knees in prayer we stand on our feet in battle in heavenly places. And to prove we believe what we say, we walk in peace with our sword raised high and our shield held in front, which pushes back the resistance. This is how we fight our battles! We trust God. Take Him at his Word. Walk by faith instead of fear. Speak the truth. Abide in His presence through prayer and we remain calm. He sends His angels to protect us, make paths and push back darkness. The Lord brings healing to our minds and allows us to see and hear what the Spirit is revealing to us. He turns around what was intended for evil and brings good out of it. Every. Single. Time.

Practically speaking, say out loud with your mouth, truth. Speak blessings. Speak of what you are grateful for and thankful for. Declare the Scriptures by reading them, or writing them in a prayer journal. If you can't do much, do as much as you can. If your mind says, "you are going to die," then you say out loud, "I am alive in Christ. I have abundant life and will live eternally because of the blood sacrifice of Jesus." If your mind says, "you are crazy!" then you say out loud, "I have the mind of Christ. He will keep in perfect peace whose mind is stayed on thee." Jesus taught us how to respond when he was tempted in the desert. Remember, the devil knows scripture but he always puts a spin on it. Do not let him use it against you. Instead, speak the Word and tell the enemy where to go! He must flee! Believe it! If Jesus himself resisted him with the Word of God, we will too. He modeled everything we need to live victorious lives but we have to apply what we know. And once you know a thing, you cannot "un-know" it. Do you know what I mean?

As I pointed out already, once we know something by experience or knowledge attained, we now have a responsibility with it. If you know your gas tank is close to empty, you are responsible to put gas in the car or you will find yourself stranded on the side of the road. If you know you have a big delivery scheduled at your house at a certain time, you must be home in time or you will not receive what you were expecting. It will be your fault if you are late and if you don't communicate a need to make a change. It is a simple cause-and-effect response to the actions taken or neglected that will bring you good or could cause you harm. If you learn this lesson through experience, you will not easily forget it. When the Lord brings revelation through your experience, you will never regret it.

Each of the four times I have suffered a short mental collapse, not only has God taught me and purified me during the process but I have learned valuable lessons from the experience. I have also gained much empathy for others while in the battle. I've allowed my heart to be pruned of false beliefs, unforgiveness, pride, hurts, trauma, anxiety, control and a lack of trust. I have also literally cleaned out many closets and drawers in my home. I have thrown many items away and made things right as a result of the pruning. Much has needed to be done in my heart as the Lord revealed thoughts, motives, idols and things that brought confusion or a separation between Him and I. But as my mind was also in a state of confusion, some of the behavior I displayed while cleaning out was in excess of what was necessary. Nonetheless, if the enemy was going to use it against me, it was going to go! I say this because I believe that good things can be tools that are used against us if we are in a vulnerable state of mind. It doesn't necessarily mean the items are evil but if they are going to serve as a reminder from the enemy to me of what I thought about during my trauma, or if they are to trigger an unhealthy emotion or reaction, I am okay with the fact that I got rid of it, irrational as the thoughts may or may not have been.

This is important to know because when your brain returns to balance and you comprehend or realize your bizarre actions and you remember the irrational thoughts (or the Holy Spirit lead thoughts) that caused you to do what you did, do not reside in regret. You may be tempted to grieve that you felt, thought or behaved the way you did, as I have. My encouragement to you is to give thanks to God that you were willing to lose stuff (if that applies) in fear of losing your soul. You were willing to do without a possession so you could live in closer fellowship with Jesus. Joy comes in the morning! Joy also comes after *mourning*! Allow the grieving process to do its work because there is joy on the other side of it. There is no shame or condemnation for those who live in Christ Jesus. So when the enemy tries to dish it up to you, just push it away, say "NO" and walk away!

Here is a practical tip as you reflect on your personal experience: own it, acknowledge it, laugh about it, cry about it, remember what you learned through it, and press on. Forget what is in the past and move forward through your present to your glorious future. It is filled with hope and healing and to be enjoyed, this side of Heaven.

Schemes revealed . . .

I will not tell you the actual lies the enemy threw at me, because I do not wish to give him any credit at all. But I will share details of a few episodes, which will serve as a reminder to me of God's faithfulness. Every lie, the Lord was with me and spoke truth to my mind and heart. I will disclose a few things so you can see clearly some of the enemy tactics. It is good to gain an understanding of your enemy so you can take him out. We are in God's army and I promise you, our national military studies the patterns of the enemy. It is what gives us advantage and allows for victory. I do wish to reveal the truth, expose the lies and equip the bride to be battle ready and not caught off guard in order to prevent casualties. The devil only comes to kill, steal and destroy, remember and it is not in his capacity to create. He attempts, though, to duplicate what is good but it always results in bad. The devil embraces the suck and tries to suck the life out of the children of God. So we will sound the alarm and tell others so they will not fall into the same traps we did. That is what brothers, sisters and friends do for one another; they serve as a hedge of protection around the family. We are the family of God and it is time we stop devouring, judging and tearing each other down. Let's get real and authentic and help each other in our times of trouble and let's celebrate with each other! In this way, we are all in this together! We are surrounded all around us by the armies of the Lord! We have an angelic force in the unseen realm that is ministering to us in our times of need and they are fighting the battles in the heavenly places, as we remain calm. The battle is the Lord's and He has won!

As I said, there were many things that actually happened that were meant to drive fear into my heart. There were also things I saw in the physical realm that were used to align with what I heard in the spiritual realm. It is not easy to talk about these things as they are not natural to our human minds and it is not something many ever experience, or at least talk about if they do. However, as I stated, there were times that words spoken were heard by my ears and perceived by my mind differently than what was voiced. Then there were other times when I heard an audible phrase that produced a manifestation of what was said in the spiritual realm. For instance, when speaking with a young neighbor, I heard this phrase audibly, "make up lies to her" then in a moment, she did. My husband was due to fly home from a business trip the following day and was unaware that I had been under a spiritual attack and suffering anxiety that week. This child came to my door after school to say hello. She inquired about Greg and I told her he would be flying home the next day. She told me about how she had never been on an airplane before. Then, right after I "heard" in the spiritual realm with my ears..."make up lies to her," she suddenly started telling this wild story of how she heard about this airplane and that her friend had accidentally gotten on the wrong flight and was heading overseas and sitting in first class. She said everyone sitting in the back was served raw chicken and was very sick. She was rambling very fast and not making any sense. A sudden chill ran down my back and a moment of fear crept in as I was being led by the liar (satan, not the child) to believe this was going to happen to my husband the next day and I was being given a clue. I recognized this as a lie and told our little friend that it was good to see her but that it was time for her to go home.

I went in the house and rebuked satan for the lie and took captive that thought, but I will tell you it brought trouble to my spirit. I knew this was a made up story and I believe she had no idea what she was saying. A sweet innocent child who is a friend was being used in attempt to stir up fear and anxiety and she had no idea. I chose to act on faith despite my troubled mind. I pretended it did not bother me, and I presented it to the Lord. I prayed for safety for my husband and the next day, I decided to act on faith and arrive early at the airport to wait in the cell phone parking lot. However, as I approached the airport, Greg called me to let me know his flight was early and I was able to pull right up and pick him up without stopping the car. Not only did he make it fine but I knew once again the Lord had helped me through the battle. When they come, you must face them with your faith. Prove you are not afraid. Move in it! Faith will rise up in you!

After picking Greg up, we went straight to one of our favorite restaurants for an early dinner and my heart was beginning to be at ease. My temporary fears of his flight had not come true and I was grateful. My faith was rising so when our waitress came to our table and I could see she had something heavy on her mind, I boldly asked her what I could pray with her about. She shared she was in an impossible situation and needed a rescue. So my husband and I agreed in prayer over her and at the moment I said, "In Jesus' name, I pray,"... a waitress behind her dropped a plate, startling the whole place. In my spirit, I felt a sense of courage arise in me, as I believe something shifted in the spiritual realm for our waitress. We prayed as unseen swords were at work clanging on behalf of her rescue and breaking chains as a result. Faith in action fills the believers heart with more faith and fills the atmosphere around us with Holy Spirit power to have faith and belief for others. I am convinced of this!

So as the enemy was working overtime to destroy my faith with fear, the Lord was increasing my faith in abundance and giving me strength. I was going to need it as my healing from this episode would take a few weeks of renewing my mind, resting, medication, the help of family, and isolation in our home from others. This was two weeks prior to the worldwide shutdown so when it came to that, I had no clue. My clueless state of mind due to an intentional time of quiet also became another tool the enemy would use to bring confusion as he matched new realities with new lies.

The Coronavirus Cover-up...

Though I was aware of the virus that had not yet hit the United States, I was unaware that during my voluntary isolation, it had indeed arrived and everything would be shutting down soon. Though I had confusion running around in my mind, I still had enough sense to notice some things and realize that something was terribly wrong. My husband started having irrational behavior. Though his actions weren't any different from the rest of the world, I was again clueless. I did not know his behavior was actually not unusual but was wisdom in action as Greg began to stock up on essentials. He is such a wonderful husband and takes great care of me. I am truly blessed and grateful for this man God matched me with. Greg is a great caretaker and he shows so much patience and love, even in sickness. We vowed to each other: in sickness and in health, and we meant it, though it was a very difficult time for Greg as he was unsure of how to help me pull out of my depression and lack of trust that had set in. Just as Greg was learning to deal with my mental imbalance episode, a worldwide crisis was emerging.

In my state of mind, imagine my surprise when suddenly, Greg, our neighbors and business partners started stocking up on paper goods, cleaning supplies, wipes, medicine, meat, milk and many other random things. They were shopping for each other and calling each other to coordinate purchases, which was completely not normal or anything I had ever witnessed. I was beginning to see things being stored in random places and stocked all over the house, including many things we already had or that I never purchased but were good staple items. Because I was the one who knew our inventory, I would get irritated with Greg that he was not consulting me on what we were out of. His careful response was that he was thinking of our extended family and neighbors in case we needed to be able to help supply food for them. This was a new thing we had never done or talked about in our years of marriage, and it was odd to me. Something weird and frightening was happening. Some of the troubling things I had seen or heard over the two-week period started to make me believe there was truth to the fears I had thought and had fought. This was real and everyone was going crazy, except me, so I argued in my unstable mind. What was happening?

Because my husband was concerned for me and was learning as he went along in this unchartered territory, Greg was trying to protect me from knowing what was going on in our world. As you and most people were aware, normal essential items were flying off the shelves as the fear of not getting them had settled in among the masses because our economy was going on shutdown. The enemy took full opportunity to launch another attack on my mind because not only was I already vulnerable, but there was a fresh reality that could be used to twist and confirm the lies. Because it involved my husband and neighbor's behavior, I felt that I was being watched all the time, though not true.

Ramped up battleground . . .

The battle in my mind quickly went to another level. I contemplated on scripture I had tucked into my heart as it came to my aid. I also relied heavily on the positive verses that were implanted on my calendars, journals, and decorations all over my house; and I listened for the voice of the Holy Spirit to speak truth to me. I was using mindless activities to reach a calm state of mind, such as adult coloring books. Some of these beautiful pages were infused with uplifting scripture as well. I would continue to journal my prayers and the Lord was faithful to speak His Word to me as I did, so I would write out scripture that the Holy Spirit would bring to my mind. But if I opened my physical Bible, I often would find myself looking at scriptures that the enemy would twist and use against me. I knew God's Word was true and powerful, but I also knew the tormenting demons are also aware of it and will try to use it against us, just like Jesus was fed the twisted Word in the desert. So I was careful not to allow it.

There were many details that I need not share as I refuse to give the enemy further ammunition by way of producing fear in others by voicing details of lies he fed me while I was down, but I want to emphasize that whatever your fears have been, or the ways the enemy has attacked you in the past, will most likely be the way he comes at you again if you become weak, weary, and lower your shield. I had watched some frightening Christian movies at church as a teenager that brought much fear for the last days on this earth. I was reminded of them. I do believe we are in the end times now, just as the disciples knew they were too as found in scriptures, but only the Father knows the full details of the very end. I believe we are to live each day as though it were our last, but plan and prepare as though it were not. I pay attention and do my best to stay alert, but I believe we are going to see and live through a great awakening and revival before that happens. However, when my mind was open to receiving ERROR messages, it played mean tricks on me. The truth is, no one knows the exact time of the Lord's return, or the details of the suffering we may go through before He does, but we do know that if we are forgiven, redeemed and in right-relationship with Jesus, to be absent in the body is to be present with Him. It is so important we keep our armor on so that we are able to recognize and reject the attacks when they come against us. My faith still holds!

I say all these things because I believe there are more people that experience these types of attacks that are not getting the real help they need. If you are having ongoing anxiety, panic attacks, or if you live a worried life, aside from the help of the Holy Spirit, it would be a good idea for you to seek professional help. I would suggest that you find someone who is grounded in the faith and who counsels based on Biblical principles. Check with your pastor or a trusted friend to seek out a referral. My heart goes out to people who suffer from mental illness and long-term effects from them. I pray the Lord pours out His Spirit upon them and brings freedom and healing to their minds, and restores their peace. That being said, it is my understanding many suffer temporary mental breakdowns, imbalances, and physical crashes because they have come under a physiological attack in their bodies that led to a spiritual attack that mimicked what many suffer constantly. I have gained so much compassion, empathy and concern for these members of our society along with the elderly as well because my experiences have given me insight.

A Walk through the Valley...to the Other Side! . . .

I have been blessed to walk through these valleys and out of them, as a stronger, wiser child of God who understands that we are not left in the valley to die and rot. The Lord walks with us, carries us, and teaches us how to thrive through the trauma valleys and then He takes us to the other side, better for it. He refines and purifies our hearts, cleanses us, gives us freedom and enables us to help His other children who need someone to come alongside them and hold their hands, validate them and point them to the hope that is available. Freely we have been given so much, so freely we should give. Our Lord gave His very life for us so we could live in freedom now as we wait an eternity of freedom in heaven. However I believe many believers in Jesus have received hope of eternal life but are living in bondage while they await their heavenly rewards. *"If the son sets you free, you shall be free indeed"* is what *John 8:36 NIV* tells me and I am living proof of it!

Joy comes in the morning! Joy also comes after mourning! Allow the grieving process to do its work because there is joy on the other side of it.

CHAPTER 5

GRIEF, GIFTS & TREASURED MEMORIES

Several gifts were granted me shortly after chemical balance returned to my brain and body. I was learning to abide in the rest of God, and retrain my mind to soak in the physical rest as well. Thanks to the shutdown, we all have been given this opportunity to slow down, take inventory of what is important, repent, heal, and spend time with loved ones. And because we truly were all in it together in this way, my temporary time of isolation went unnoticed to most because they too were isolated. I am grateful for the gifts of time and rest, but there were two other gifts the Lord gave me that was significant in my healing. They came in the form of two preachers that were able to help me receive inner healing/deliverance, and practical help that would give me wisdom and knowledge to not put my body in a place of vulnerability again. You do not know what you do not know but once you know, you can't "un-know" what you now know. Whew! That was a mouthful but reread it if you must. Once you have revelation or understanding of how you may live free and healed, you have personal responsibility to heed the revelation. I've been given this knowledge from someone who understood first hand what I had experienced and why it was allowed to happen. I also recognize it does not ever have to happen again and I am no longer afraid, thanks be to God. In the reverse order I received them, let me tell you about the gifts, Rev. Jay and Pastor Ron.

The second gift/person to help me was Jay Jellison. He and his wife currently run the Iron Acres Ranch just outside of Topeka, KS which is used for ministering to couples, families, pastors, ministry leaders and organizations who wish to take a respite break to hear from the Lord, heal relationships and abide in the holy rest of God. Jay and his wife Judy also share in their gift of discipleship, deliverance and healing ministries, among other areas the Lord is using them to grow the Kingdom of God. Jay was referred to us initially because some people dear to us thought Greg and I both would benefit from the deliverance and healing ministry they offer. We were learning to navigate our way out of the trauma we had both suffered. We made a call to Jay, and he did not believe we needed deliverance but would benefit from coming to the ranch and staying in the Bed & Breakfast on the property, as well as having a few sessions with him. It was set and we were able to go and be refreshed, hear from the Lord, receive some revelation and confirmation on some things and further our healing. But one of the greatest benefits that came from this new relationship was learning that Jay had knowledge, experience and understanding regarding the physiological and spiritual attacks I had suffered each of the four times. The wisdom he gave me carried hope with it!

I learned that I, like him, have at times suffered from a rush of cortisol to our brains when we've allowed our bodies to be worn down to the point of total exhaustion. Jay compared his past experience with mine and said, "The rush of cortisol carried by adrenalin actuates our limbic system, throws our bodies into a state of imbalance, and causes the body to enter into a limbic cycle. This cycle causes the brain to see three options for survival, fight-flight-or-freeze, and it happens for no apparent reason. This limbic cycle triggers anxiety to come to the surface." I had NEVER heard this before even though I've seen doctors and have received counseling. It made so much sense to me and I was soaking in everything Jay told me about it as I was feeling a sense of relief there was scientific information and help. The limbic system, located in the brain, controls some behaviors that are essential to life, such as motivation and emotional behaviors, and if there was past trauma, some of the behaviors and new fears are tied to survival and avoidance of repeat events. Its function is important to the body so I've been researching to learn more about the limbic system because I need to maintain its health, as I know firsthand what it is like when mine gets hijacked. I've included a link on the bibliography source page to a very informative article written by the Institute for Restorative Health. If you believe you may suffer from an impaired limbic system occasionally, please read it and know there is help available.

As a personal result of this physiological response, the serotonin in my brain has gotten backed up in the past and won't release without the help of a medication, combined with exercise, rest and mental relaxation. For me, each time it has hit this level, I have been prescribed a medication for a month or two. Shortly after we begin the meds and let them take effect, we begin the slow weaning off process. I am truly grateful for medications when needed, though I usually turn to natural remedies for cures and prevention. I also learned that when our bodies become out of whack like mine had, it opens up the door for the enemy to attack us spiritually while we are down. We usually don't even realize we are suffering until it hits the spiritual attack level, thereby hitting us by a complete surprise. But every single time I have experienced this same physical and mental crash, not only have there been similarities in my experiences, but I can also see the pattern that took place that preceded the personal pandemic. Clues have been left, and now thanks to my new friend, I can see it clearly. I realize I have personal responsibility to take care of my body and not get to a place of extreme exhaustion. And if beyond my control it should occur, or if I should ignore the wisdom I have received and allow myself to go there, it is certainly not the time to enter into spiritual warfare through intense intercessory prayer. It is time to take a break, rest, and request personal prayer coverage from prayer warrior friends. I also know that past patterns need not be repeated because I can learn to create a new narrative in my brain to lean on as a default. What we speak, believe, meditate and rely on becomes our "go to" when we are in trouble so it is important to prepare when in a state of calm so calamity doesn't hit when chaos arises. As a result, we will be in control and in a much better place mentally because we are no longer okay with a hijack of our mind.

You've been warned . . .

Learning to distinguish the warning signs will help to recognize when it's time to slow down. The signs vary from chronic fatigue, irritability, slowed responses and problems making decisions, among others. You would think you would automatically realize you are at a critical point, but often we are so engrossed in what we are doing and we put pressure on ourselves to do the things we set out to do, that we do not realize we are approaching danger. It is important to give permission to your loved ones to pay attention and help guide you when they see you are perhaps not thinking or acting like yourself. Try to be patient with them and not get defensive as they truly are looking out for your best interest. If this happens, try to thank your loved one for noticing and perhaps take a break, or go to bed early so you can get a fresh start the next day with a clear mind. Consider the gift of wisdom you just received from me and take heed.

If I am suffering from grief, not dealt with from the past, or if a new wave of grief enters my life through personal loss, this is also not the time to sign up to do prophetic activation, intercessory prayer or other activities that would cause my body to become weary. These are also some of the situations that have accompanied the fatigue for me personally that preceded a mental breakdown. In addition, deep grief had been present prior to a spiritual high, and weariness tagged along for the ride. Do not "...*become weary in doing good...*" spoken in *Galatians 6:9 NIV*, takes on a whole new meaning to me now. I used to think this scripture's meaning was: do not become weary OF doing good; as in don't get tired of doing good. I do believe that is one interpretation, but I also understand it now to mean: while doing good, do not allow yourself to become weary in the process. Your health matters and if you are not taking care of your body, you may not be up to any good, or able to do good. So, watch out not to get out of balance so you may continue to "do good."

The key is to not allow the cortisol buildup in the body to get out of balance. Knowledge brings responsibility. I wish to stay healthy and maintain balance. I owe this not only to the Lord and my family, but to myself as well and I am compelled to tell you. You picked up this book for a reason, and perhaps you have just received an "aha moment" of insight too. I am grateful!

That explains so much . . .

This Holy Spirit guided gift of scientific knowledge and understanding has brought so much peace to my mind. It has validated my experiences and has attached a viable explanation to it, as well as a remedy. I believe this wisdom has also helped my family tremendously. Not that I am happy someone else has suffered similar to my experience, as I do not wish it on anyone, but knowing this gave me hope and made me feel I was not alone. I was made aware because someone was willing to be vulnerable enough to share that he identified with what I had been through. I realize I must do the same as it opens doors for healing for others when I express and share from my own experiences. Perhaps you have felt alone and in reading this, though your encounters may not be exactly like mine, you have wondered what was wrong with you and if you were ever going to be well. I am here to tell you, there is hope and there is healing for you! Before I received this gift from Jay, I did indeed receive the gift of inner healing and deliverance as I was gifted a treasured time with another who passed away two weeks after our divine appointment. Pastor Ron Frizzel was another gift to me and I will be eternally grateful.

A priceless gift in the Zoom Room . . .

Though we had not met in person, I was familiar with Pastor Ron through mutual friends who had received personal deliverance ministry and an impartation of the anointing he carried. I was looking forward to the day I too would meet him. Eight months before our

Zoom online meeting, I was privileged to hear him share his testimony and preach at the final "Awakening" gathering held in Fort Worth, Texas, the fall of 2019. I took many notes from the wisdom he shared and the richness it brought to me. I also found out he was the father of one of my favorite Christian singer/ songwriter/ worship leaders, Steffany Gretzinger. As I have been encouraged through her worship, my thoughts were that her parents had obviously raised her in a spirit-filled, loving environment and I was even more excited about the day we would meet Ron and Kathy Frizell, as our friends had mentioned we would. I did not expect that I would be meeting Ron over a 3-hour Zoom, 1,000 miles away from each other, in the middle of a worldwide pandemic. Of course this year, the only thing we have been able to expect has truly been the unexpected. I also did not expect that I would receive such powerful inner healing from this divine appointment either, but that's exactly what I received.

Ron listened to my candid detailed story and did not judge, but rather heard me with compassion and understanding. He completely understood me and was not surprised by the details I shared with him regarding not only the spiritual attacks I had suffered, but also the grief I had endured throughout my life. I told him everything without holding back because I knew the Holy Spirit had set this appointment in order and that Pastor Ron heard the Spirit clearly and could help me. I recognized the holy moment the Lord had arranged and I was not going to miss the opportunity to receive all He had in store for my life. I was done with the cycle of torment and was ready to be open to respond so I could be fully healed. I told him everything.

The traumatic memory of our accident . . .

I told of the tragic sudden loss of my 34 year-old mother Barbara and 5 year-old sister, Jennifer, in a car wreck my family was in when I was 14 years old. My father, Brance, and 12 year old sister, Melodi and I miraculously survived after being T-boned by a car traveling 70 miles an hour that had run a stop sign on July 3, 1980 just before midnight. The teenage driver was under the influence of alcohol and was running from the police. He went to jail for 6 months and was let off on a suspended sentence because proper tests and searches were not done at the scene of the accident. This was a traumatic time in my life and brought great grief into it as you can imagine.

I recalled to Ron how just a few months after the accident my father was engaged to marry a friend of our family who had been my Sunday school teacher when I was young. She had never married, and on a trip to hold a revival, my dad passed through our old hometown in Texas and he met her and other longtime friends for dinner. He went on to preach in south Texas, and on the way home stopped to visit our friend, and proposed to her. They were married nine months later and continue to share a beautiful marriage now 39 years later.

Connie has been a wonderful grandma to our kids and she holds a special place in my heart today. I am grateful the Lord provided her to my dad and to our family. She was an answer to dad's prayers and a real help to our family who was suffering the senseless loss of Mom and Jennifer. Connie had been a good friend of my mom and that brought me comfort. Though my sister and I were happy our dad had found love again, the timing of it all was very difficult for us as you might imagine. As young teenage girls with much loss, we were barely into the second stage of grief when the process was interrupted.

Stuck in a grief cycle ...

There are several common emotional stages of grief that most everyone experiences usually, though not always, in this order: shock (or disbelief), denial, bargaining, guilt, anger, depression, and acceptance (which includes hope). The symptoms manifest in different ways and can be emotional or physical when they do. The stages may, for different reasons, be out of order or combined, or if the process is not allowed, the stages can be blocked for a time. This is what happened to me and I was completely unaware of it. I tried to be happy for our dad as he was moving forward, and on my face, I was, but down deep inside of my core, I was in deep sorrow. I had just lost my mom and baby sister. Everything had changed in an instant as I was beginning High School and learning to live without them. We had to move forward, and with undesirable circumstances, my grief process was like a record player stuck on the song titled "Denial." It was easier to just let it go, look to the future, and stuff the grief and trauma as a way of survival. These thoughts and feelings were not calculated and I didn't even realize what was happening, but my emotional autopilot took over and in less than a year from the accident, we had a new family dynamic, a new home in a new state, a new school, a new church, new friends and a new normal. Anytime you have two or more big changes in your life at once, stress accompanies it. But if you are stuffing it, you just add another invisible layer that will reveal itself at a later unexpected time.

The move back to Texas was good for our family in numerous ways and many blessings came from it. With all the immediate unexpected changes, this was truly a traumatic time but it was also a terrific time in my life. My sister, Melodi and I became very close and we relied on each other. She and I welcomed a new baby sister, Kristin, two years later after I began my senior year. She brought joy to our lives and continues to do so, as we have all three settled in the same city as adults. I am grateful for my two sisters and I believe in Melodi, Kristin and in the love we share. I look forward to the day we are reunited with our sister Jennifer and my precious mom, Grandma Barbara, as my children refer to her.

The dream "gift" of my mom . . .

Many milestones had taken place in my life soon after our move back to San Antonio. In that three year period, I had started my first real job, bought my first car, begun to drive, began dating, and was now preparing to graduate High School and make the move back to Oklahoma to begin college. I desired so much to spend some time with my mom and tell her all about everything going on in my life, as most teenage girls do.

One night, the Lord gave me a beautiful gift I will never forget. It was a very vivid dream where I was driving my new (new to me) car down a road I traveled on daily from my home to go anywhere. All of the sudden, I spotted my mom on the side of the road waiting, as if she were a hitch-hiker, though she was waiting for me. She was so excited to see me. I gave her a ride and poured out my heart to her.

As I drove her around town, she listened mostly and let me know how happy she was for me and how proud she was of me. And then she said, "Suzanne, this is where I need to get out of the car." I pulled over and then we embraced and told how much we loved each other before she made her exit. As I was pulling away, I glanced in the rearview mirror to see her one more time, but she was already gone. I awakened with a full heart, knowing I had received a huge blessing from the Lord, and I was truly grateful for the supernatural encounter I had received while I slept.

When I woke up, the bottled up tension in my heart was relieved. Even though I only spoke to mom in my dream, I was able to talk about everything, which was necessary to receive the relief. It is important to talk to someone you know, trust and can share your heart with. This was a lesson I would one day get, though it would take a while to resonate with me. Confession is good for the soul. We are told we need to confess our sins to each other and pray for one another so we may be healed, according to *James 5:16*. But I believe confessing our inner hurts, feelings, and thoughts to someone who will listen to you, love you and pray for you, also brings healing. The Lord often gives us wisdom, discernment, deliverance, healing, godly counsel and direction through others when we do. He speaks to us through His Word, His Spirit, and through His people.

The gift of "gab" . . .

Back in the eighties, counselors and mentors were not discussed much. I do not recall the thought of "talking to someone" even being considered, or crossing anyone's mind. Today, when a family member or close friend goes through grief or trauma, or if they are having a difficult time dealing with someone or something, we immediately think to make sure we provide professional counseling or we find them someone they can talk to. It is essential to our overall physical, emotional and spiritual health and healing. We also now understand the importance of authentic relationships and creating safe spaces within our own homes to talk about our feelings and discuss areas in which we are in need of healing. This can be a humbling experience as the topic of discussion may include something you have personally allowed or done that has brought pain to someone you love. Perhaps there is bitterness, offense or confusion in the relationship that needs to be addressed, but when you humble yourself before the Lord, He will lift you up! Humility activates forgiveness and restoration. It produces the fruit of love, peace, hope and joy and it leads to healing!

Jesus makes all things new! He turns our messes into messages. He heals the deep wounds of our memories. He gives good gifts to His children. Often, the best gift He provides proves to be one of His other children ready to listen, ready to gab and ready to give you their time, attention and wisdom. Who knew the gift of gab could truly be a treasured gift from the Lord, but it has been for me and I am of course eternally grateful.

> *Humility activates forgiveness and restoration. It produces the fruit of love, peace, hope and joy and it leads to healing!*

CHAPTER 6

GOOD GRIEF – THERE'S MORE?

When the grief process gets blocked, the healing is delayed - for a time. Symptoms of the blockage may emerge regardless of your awareness, such as you being easily hurt, fearful, having feelings of rejection or abandonment, over-achieving, or striving to fit in or control situations as a means of protection. Your actions and reactions due to these feelings build a false belief system in your inner being in which you operate and judge from, and in which you believe to be normal. This false belief system takes root in your life and begins to grow deeper into your heart, at your very core. These "weeds" need to be dealt with or they will become sources of problems in your future and at some unexpected point, they will spring up to the surface and deal with you. Trust me, it is better to pull up the weeds rather than to spend your life in constant weed management. That's exhausting and ineffective.

Deal with the Roots . . .

"Deal with the roots or the roots will deal with you." This is what Rev. Ron Frizzell said to me as I relayed some background details to my life story. He began to ask me questions that took me back to my beginnings, including what was going on in the life of my mother while she carried me in her womb. I opened up and told him everything I could remember and what I was aware of as best as I could.

Over the past twenty-five years, I have met with Spirit-filled pastors and wives, counselors, mentors, and friends for the sake of confession, prayer, wisdom and healing. I have also allowed the Holy Spirit to reveal and expose my heart for correction, restoration and renewing my mind. I have walked the process of forgiving my husband, my father, and the driver of the car who caused our fatal accident. I have forgiven myself and have received the forgiveness of Jesus; I have confessed my hidden sins to God and man, have repented, and have experienced great mercy and grace from God. As a whole, the Lord has restored our marriage, our family and His peace in my life. So why have I had to deal with four mental and physical crashes over the past sixteen years? I believe it is because there was deep inner healing and deliverance work the Lord wanted to do in my heart. Hence, the questions Pastor Ron asked relaying back to my birth and a recalling of some early childhood experiences that had brought a belief system in my mind that I could not trust men. I also had developed a belief system that skewed my view of leaders in ministry in regards to their priorities as relating to their families. I learned that some beliefs are learned and some are passed down through DNA from generation to generation, often referred to as a generational curse, but this can be stopped and reversed. If agreement created the problem, a new agreement can create the resolve!

Powered by the Holy Spirit, Ron discerned much and was able to walk me through deliverance from the bondage of evil created through my agreement with these false beliefs. I had indeed experienced real traumatic things in my life that produced these beliefs, so in that regard, it was understandable; however, Jesus gave His life so I would be free, not just saved. He saved my soul when I accepted Jesus Christ as my Savior, into my heart. He cleansed me from sin and gave me

His righteousness and put His spirit in me when I received His gift of forgiveness. But I was not walking in total freedom because my mind still needed to be renewed. But in the meantime, prior to being delivered, my mind periodically had become the battleground for a demonic attack on my body as I have mentioned already.

Walking in our authority . . .

With my voice, I chose to literally break the bond of agreement with lies the enemy had me chained to. As believers in Jesus Christ, as found in *Luke 10:19*, we have been given power and authority OVER all the powers of the enemy and of the darkness. We have to exercise it though or the power switch never gets turned on. The enemy will take advantage of every opportunity we give him to keep us feeling defeated and destroyed. But Jesus came to destroy all the works of the devil and that He did, on the cross. One of the ways that truth becomes a reality in our lives is when we believe it and walk in it. We are to walk with the belt of truth securely fitted around our waist to hold us together. When we are walking with the lie tied around our core, we begin to fall apart. We have to pull ourselves together and tighten up the belt of truth and make sure we put on the full armor of God so we can stand firm.

Our part is to trust the process Jesus puts in motion when we receive Him as our Lord and Savior. Sometimes people are instantly freed from addictions and habits, and sometimes, they have to walk it out. Grief and trauma seem to usually require the longer process towards inner healing, but when we recognize who we are and Whose we are in Christ, the pace can be sped up and not have to drag out a lifetime. So if you are realizing by the Holy Spirit speaking to your heart that perhaps you have some health issues that may relate to some spiritual issues you have not come to terms with yet, I would encourage you to seek help. Seek out a Christian counselor, a deliverance ministry or a trusted friend who is walking in close fellowship with the Holy Spirit to meet with. Ask the Lord to direct your steps and divinely introduce you to the ones He wants to align you to, but you must begin to seek help. If you seek help, you will find it so be careful where you look. Not all help is created equal.

Begin to forgive and live forgiven . . .

The best place to get your needed relief over grief is at the foot of the cross. Seek the face of Jesus and call upon Him to be your help. He meets all of our needs and His Spirit will speak to your spirit and be your guide. If you are not already aware, ask the Lord to reveal to you anyone in whom you need to seek forgiveness or in whom you need to forgive. Forgiveness is a key that opens up the door for deliverance and freedom in your heart. It is why Jesus said, as recorded in *Matthew 5:23 NIV, "Therefore, if you are offering your gift at the altar and there remember that your brother or sister has something against you, leave your gift there in front of the altar. First go and be reconciled to them; then come and offer your gift."* The Lord forgives us our sins as a free gift but as we have received forgiveness so freely, so freely we must also forgive, or as the Word says, there is no forgiveness of sins for ourselves. He takes this seriously and we are unable to walk in freedom unless we reconcile our differences, restore relationships, love each other and let go of grudges, bitterness or offense, moment-by-moment and day-by-day!

You may be thinking it's easier said than done and I would agree. In the natural realm, and in our own strength, it is impossible to truly forgive. But that is the beauty of the Holy Spirit working in and through our lives as we submit to Him. Paul quotes Jesus in response to his pleading to be rid of a thorn in his flesh. We read in *2 Corinthians 12:9 ESV, "But he said to me, "My grace is sufficient for you, for my power is made perfect in weakness."* Paul shares of delighting in his troubles, persecutions and in difficulties and proclaims in *verse 10, "For when I am weak, then I am strong."* He said this because in and of ourselves, we are too weak and unable to do the things that bring everlasting change in our hearts. We need the help and power of the Holy Spirit to act on our behalf but this only happens when we surrender ourselves to Him. We, in our sinful nature, are selfish and prideful and want people to pay the price for the harm they have caused us. We sometimes want what David often called for in the Psalms, for God to destroy our enemies and recompense us for what was stolen. We want revenge and we want to wallow in self-pity (which is pride by the way) and we want to make our perpetrators suffer. I know I at least have felt this way in the past. I can relate to David, can you?

Faithful, or not! . . .

Sixteen years into my now almost thirty-three years of marriage, when I discovered that the "ties that bind us" had been torn and that trust had been broken, I became weak and weary. I grieved the loss of what I thought I had, a faithful faith-filled marriage. I had seen the signs and rode the roller coaster for years, but did not want to see the truth for fear of what I would find. For years, I had prayed for my husband, and for a break of the secret bondage he had with pornography. I prayed he'd be the man I had sought to marry who would lead our family in the ways of the Lord. I desired to have a spiritual leader as a lifetime partner who would take up the shield of faith and grow with me. I had come to the conclusion that it was better to pretend things were okay and co-exist for the sake of our children than for us to confess our sins, confront our issues, and let the Lord take control of the outcome.

I was afraid. I did not want to be a divorced single mom of three and I did not want to live with the reality of what I could not change, so I chose the path of intentional ignorance. I'm not recommending this path, but just owning up to what happened to me. Yet, I continued to pray for a change and for my husband's deliverance from the bondage of sexual sin. His parents were also aware of Greg's struggles and had sought the Lord for help for years. Our prayers matter and make a difference. Help was on the way!

The near miss collision in mid-air . . .

When people pray and stand in the gap for others, things shift in answer to prayers. My husband was tired of living a lie but did not know how to change. He wanted to feel better but did not want to give up his lifestyle. As a pilot, he found himself in a near miss mid-air collision, in a small private airplane. Six months later after a radical change in his life, he admitted he knew that if he had died that day, he would have been eternally lost. Pornography introduced to him as a young teenage boy, established a pattern of behaviors that took him down a deep dark road set before him by his own evil desires and guided by the enemy of his soul. *James 1:13-15 NIV says, "When tempted, no one should say, "God is tempting me." For God cannot be tempted by evil, nor does he tempt anyone; but each person is tempted when they are dragged away by their own evil desire and enticed. Then, after desire has conceived, it gives birth to sin; and sin, when it is full-grown, gives birth to death."*

Greg felt trapped and sensed he had a permanent thorn in his flesh as Paul did. I recently heard that when a young teenage brain is exposed to images of pornography, it has the same effect as crack cocaine. It is highly addictive and usually leads to a lifetime of addictive behaviors. This had been Greg's case and now, as an adult, he was weak and in need of the miracle working power of the Holy Spirit to move in his life.

An honest prayer to be humbled . . .

Greg was grateful he was alive when the plane safely landed, but as he recalls, he was not ready to make a change. He knew he needed to and he wanted to "want to" but at that time, the evil desires were stronger than his desires to adjust his lifestyle. So he prayed the only thing he thought to pray, "Lord, humble me." Before we go on, the Lord has shown me that it was the prayers of Greg's parents joined with my own prayers for years that allowed Greg to be inspired to pray for personal humility. One living in deep sin does not usually ask God to humble him. The power of praying for your loved ones is effective when done from a position of fervent righteous humility in anguish for the soul of the lost. Do not give up and do not get discouraged because the Lord is working all things out in His timing to bring answers to your prayers, especially when it involves the rescue of souls. Keep watch and keep praying.

For six months, Greg prayed this secret prayer and eventually began to truly desire to change. His persistence to be humbled got the Lord's attention, and finally one night, the eve of my birthday, the Lord broke His silence and spoke to Greg's heart. He asked him this question, "Greg, do you really want to change?" Greg's answer was a solid "Yes!" to which the Lord replied a succession of things Greg might be forced to give up if he repented and confessed. To be a man of integrity, which was Greg's desire, things were going to be exposed, revealed and confronted and it was going to cause pain. He would be at the mercy of loved ones whom he would seek forgiveness and make restitution to. I was not the only one he would have to humble himself before. He told the Lord he was ready and asked God to help him change.

The turnaround . . .

The next morning when he woke up, he checked an email from his Dad with the subject line that read: Greg, I need to talk to you about some changes. When he read the heading, the Holy Spirit immediately whispered, "Today is the day you come clean!" It was an intense command and Greg knew his obedience would be hurtful on his wife's birthday, but he also knew as he argued with God on the timing of this day, that he was at a crossroads and in danger of grieving the Holy Spirit. He heard in his spirit that if he did not repent this day, that he never would. It frightened Greg and he knew he was in desperate need of help! He called upon a dear friend, a godly man, a Christian counselor, Dan Palmer, in whom he would confide in, confess to and solicit godly wisdom and counsel. Prayer had made this possible.

The full story with greater details of how everything unfolded is found at the end of this book by way of a link to hear our spoken testimony, but what I want to share now is that when Greg was weak and he called upon the Lord for help, the Holy Spirit responded. Greg had to come to a place in his life where he was most concerned about his relationship with his Maker than he was with anyone else. Greg was experiencing true godly sorrow. He was broken, or poor in spirit, and was grieving how he had turned his back on God and had hurt Him. He was sorrowful for his willful sin and for not living a righteous life. He had taken the gift of salvation he had received at a young age and tossed it aside and now he felt a deep sorrow and remorse in his heart. He wanted Jesus to be Lord of his life and he knew it would cost him. It's at this place of total surrender to God that we find He reaches down from Heaven with an extended arm and places His hand upon our hearts. He responds to our repentance. He responds to our humility. *"Blessed are the poor in spirit, for theirs is the Kingdom of Heaven!" Matthew 5:3 ESV.* I've heard you can replace the words, "the poor in spirit" for "those who are humble." Blessed are those who are humble, for the Kingdom of Heaven belongs to them. True humility leads to godly sorrow—to repentance—to salvation—to a changed life—with no regrets! God was answering our prayers! Which ones? All of them!

Confess and be healed . . .

Greg's confession was released in a progressive manner. Due to the depth of sin and the people he needed to go to in a certain order, there was a delay in me hearing the whole truth. It was also the Christmas season and Greg did not want to ruin our focus on Jesus any further, so he carefully disclosed some of the details early in December, and the rest after the holidays.

During the four weeks of initial discovery, the Lord also began a new work on my own heart. I was hurt and feeling everything I had described to you earlier about wanting to be paid back for what had been done to me. I was happy that God had answered my prayers and Greg truly was showing he was a changed man. He was acting different than I had ever seen him and was humble, and owning up to everything. He was not making excuses and he was showing signs of truly seeking God. He was happy! I was happy that he was happy but because Greg had a clean mind meant that I now had a dirty one. His dirt was dumped on me with new knowledge I received with his confession. It was messy!

I became angry as I realized the things the Lord told him he might have to give up were also things that would affect me. My pretend security rug was getting pulled out from under me and I was not happy about it. In my prideful attitude, I told the Lord that it was not fair because I was the "good one, the faithful one, the right one," and was being punished for his wrongs. That is when the Lord answered me loud and clear with this message, "I am dealing with Greg's heart. Now, let's take a look at yours." Ouch! I knew exactly what He meant and I hit the closet floor with my face to the carpet in humility. The first thing I would confess was my ugly pride.

I cried out to the Lord to forgive me and to show me everything He wanted to. I confessed bitterness and allowed the Lord to walk me through forgiving the men who had hurt me. I also needed to be truthful and confess some things to Greg that I had hidden in my heart from him. As the Lord began to remind me of things, I requested he take me on the journey to get it all done. I did not want to stay on the emotional roller coaster any longer. Since Greg was obviously on the track going the right way, I wanted to get on it too, so that we would not crisscross our tracks and get derailed. This was an opportunity to receive healing in my heart and in our marriage but it was going to cost me as well. I was willing to pay up.

I had to get real and raw and I too would join Greg and begin making restitution for wrongs I had done in my life. I know some things we can just let go of as we repent, mature, grow and go along in life, but when you have lived in a place where the enemy has kept you in bondage and afraid of telling the truth, it is only the truth that will set you free. I was not about to give the devil anything to hold over my head to bring up at a later opportune time and Greg wasn't either. We knew who our real enemy was and we were in agreement to expel him from our marriage, our family and our home. We had to take this seriously.

That Christmas season, we were both turning our eyes and our hearts towards God. Jesus had done so much for us and we were thankfully worshipping Him! He was doing a brand new thing in us individually and in our marriage. I was moved to tell Greg that though I did not know exactly what he had done but knew I would soon find out, I was choosing to forgive him. I was taking an initial step of faith as God was walking me through the process of personal healing and learning to trust in Him. In that moment, it was a blind step of faith to forgive but my eyes would soon be opened after the holiday celebrations and I would have to make another choice that could alter our future and would potentially shape the futures of our children and future generations. Our choices matter and they affect others.

Choose to Forgive . . .

A few days after Christmas, I would hear specifics that would leave me numb and in a state of weakness as I pondered what choice I would make in light of new information. Would I remain faithful to my choice to forgive or would I give up? Paul's words, "In my weakness, He is strong," would come to play out in my life as well. When I was at my weakest point, I called out to the Lord and He answered me. I told the Lord He could speak through me, as I had no words to say to my husband because I was deeply hurt. I literally asked the Holy Spirit to fill my mouth with His words. Shortly after, Greg came to me weeping, and said, "Suzanne, my tears are not for me but for the hurt and pain I have caused you. I don't even know how to ask you to forgive me!" With that, I instinctively pulled Greg close and said these shocking words, "I love you Greg and I choose to forgive you!" I did not plan to say that but I did plan to be a vessel the Lord could communicate through. I gave Him permission to speak through me to Greg, what I could not speak without Him. When He speaks...He creates!

That day, He created an environment in our hearts where He could begin a new work in our marriage. It would take time and it would reveal more truths we would have to deal with. The restoration of our relationship would require intensive counseling and a long term counselor who would teach us and guide us to work on creating a healthy marriage. It would require time to build trust again. This newly created space would also provide a place where I could set up an environment of trust to allow Greg to prove to be a man of integrity. This new climate created by the Holy Spirit's words, would require a total dependence upon Him to finish the work He began in me. The forgiveness words that poured out of my mouth had to be practiced so that my actions and attitude matched my declaration. I had to rely on the Lord's strength more than ever as we were entering into new territory. The Lord was pouring His joy upon our heads and we began to realize the joy of the Lord truly is our strength.

The Lord heals what time reveals . . .

Eventually we would receive our healing in its fullness, and years later, our grown children would too. Over time, we would witness the change in atmosphere in our home as Greg was living a life of integrity and taking up the spiritual leadership I had always longed for. I was growing in grace and learning how to allow Greg to lead, and learning the art of submission. That was a miracle in itself as I have a strong independent personality.

Years later, when appropriate, we revealed our past and confessed to our children the truth of what had taken place in our home when they were younger and how the Lord had rescued, restored and healed. This truth brought clarity to confusion and it also brought a new set of emotions and behaviors as our children had to process and walk out their own individual paths towards forgiveness and freedom. It was not easy for any of us, but the Lord is faithful and His ways are higher than ours. The path to freedom was never promised to be easy, but it was promised to be fruitful when we abide in Christ and walk in obedience to Him. His timing and order is best and what He allows us to go through is not to harm us but to cleanse us, purify our hearts and prepare us for what He knows lies ahead in our future. The cycle had to be broken for the sake of our family. In all ways, my hope and trust is in God alone! He is a good, good Father!

After the holidays, "It" happened . . .

With that in mind, my heart and my mind were in turmoil shortly after devastating details were delivered after Christmas. It was now early January of 2005 and Greg and I were riding on a spiritual high because the Lord was restoring so many things. As I began this book telling you, the Holy Spirit had instructed me to begin prayer journaling mid December. I was learning to be intimate with the Lord and pour out my heart to Him. At this vulnerable time in my life, He was the only one I felt I could trust. My distrust of men was fueled in that I believed they all had secret lives, which I know is not true. But this is where my mind was at that time.

God was answering many of our prayers, and drawing Greg and I closer to each other. We were experiencing miracles and encounters during the day and then sharing them late with each other into the late night hours. This habit was affecting my sleep. I would wake up before dawn and journal my thoughts and prayers, then take care of the kids during the day. I was riding on the excitement of what God was doing in our hearts, but then I would get hit with enormous emotion from the reality of what we had just come through.

The weight of the knowledge was heavy on me and I was in tandem, grieving from the emotional and mental trauma I had just suffered. I began to doubt my ability to trust in anyone except God because certainly if I were capable of it, I thought I would surely have seen through the lies we had been living. So, I began doubting if this new life of truth was real. I would dialogue it out in my mind and think of the "what ifs." I entertained thoughts instead of capturing them and making them obedient to Christ. I began allowing mental movies to consume me and fear began to settle in. I gave the devil an opportunity and he took it.

I would later discover through our counselor friend, Dan Palmer, that the physiological height of emotion you rise to will be the same distance below the balanced line that you fall if and when you come crashing down. Because my emotions were at an all time high regarding this change of behavior, I was at risk. My hope in restoration was high and the spiritual growth I was personally experiencing was greater than I could comprehend. I was taken emotionally to great heights. This high followed the deepest low I had ever felt in my life when I was blindsided with the truth of the sin that had been present for years prior to December 6, 2004. I was ripe to take the plunge on the coaster to an even deeper dark place, and my body gave way to the ride. I had never been on this kind of ride before and I got thrown from the tracks with the first ever shockwave of panic, anxiety, depression and crippling fear. Everything I had ever known before paled to this dark presence and frightening time in my life.

Forgiveness is a key that opens up the door for deliverance and freedom in your heart.

CHAPTER 7

MELTDOWN AFTER MOURNING

The first time I ever experienced a physical and mental meltdown in my life was a few weeks into January of 2005. Overnight, my body literally gave out and crashed, leaving me unable to function. I stayed in my bed for weeks, was immediately filled with irrational fear, and I lost my appetite and desire to do anything. Depression and anxiety settled upon me as my mind began to play tricks on me. I suddenly was gripped with fear and mistrust of everyone. One of my dear friends had experienced something similar after the loss of her best friend, and she knew exactly what to do as she had received proper medical attention at her time of need. She came to Greg's aid and connected us with her doctor who was able to fill the prescriptions, give Greg counsel and keep me from going to the mental hospital. I am grateful, as this was a temporary physical issue that could be corrected. But I was also suffering a temporary spiritual issue as I was being attacked in my mind. I was unable to read the Bible because just like the enemy twisted God's spoken words to Adam & Eve and twisted the written Word to Jesus, when tempting them, he was doing the same to me. It brought sudden confusion to my spirit, so I avoided reading it.

Though I couldn't read the written Word, I knew the Word deep in my heart because I had tucked it deep within my spirit since I was a little girl. I had memorized scripture, knew songs that were full of the Word of God, and I knew the Truth lived within me. I also knew Jesus was the Word of God. I knew that He, the Word, became flesh and dwelt among us. I knew that Jesus, when He ascended to Heaven, sent His Holy Spirit to abide in the hearts of all who received Jesus as Lord and Savior. I knew the Holy Spirit is alive and speaks to hearts, as He had to mine so often. I knew that the living Word of God also knew the written Word of God and could speak it to my heart, even if I had not memorized it. Miraculously, I still trusted God. Our lives are like sponges and when we are squeezed, what we are filled with is what comes out.

People were praying for me and their prayers activated in me a desire to ask the Lord to remind me of all scriptures, songs, poems, and truths I needed to hear at just the right time in response to every lie the devil presented to me, so I could resist him. He did just that. I wish I had recorded them at that time, but the Lord was faithful to His Word and He delivered what I needed right on time, every time. He is so awesome and wonderful!

I also began to ask the Holy Spirit to teach me and help me to escape the fear and depression I was experiencing. He is the best teacher and is ready to be your help in times of trouble when you ask Him to. Do you reject your kids asking for your help and assistance when they are afraid or don't know what to do? Of course not! Parents delight in offering help to our children, unless it is of course to get one more drink of water way past bedtime. Ha-ha! The Lord also delights in us when we call upon Him, anytime of the day or night! He is our living drink of water we really do need. He sends His own Spirit to come to our aid. The Lord came to my rescue and helped me see hope was rising up. I began to get inspired to do a few tangible things that helped me in the healing process. God heals, but he requires us to participate in it. Get up! Take up your mat! Walk!

Let the Healing begin . . .

The Lord inspired me to get out a clean sheet of paper and draw a line down the middle of it. On one side, I was instructed to list all the things that I was angry about, including the things that irritated me about my husband. Then, on the other side of the line, I was told to list everything I was grateful for but it had to include things I was thankful for that I saw in Greg. At first, the complaint list was really long but as I reluctantly wrote out my grateful words, I soon had a longer list of things I was able to say thank you for. I was grateful that Greg was a good provider for our family, that he loved our children well, and that he had a sense of humor. I was grateful he had turned his heart towards the Lord and that he was working on being a better husband.

I listed many things I was thankful for, and as I continued to write, my heart started to wake up and place a smile on my face. You see, when you are focused fully on yourself and in the sad situation you find yourself in, your gaze causes you to remain in a depressed state of mind. But when you take over those thoughts and make them obedient to Christ by dwelling on things that are lovely, admirable and praiseworthy, you snuff out destructive lingering logic and you begin to renew your mind. The Bible is true and full of wisdom and counsel and when applied to your life, brings new life to your soul. We are told in Romans to be transformed by the renewing of our minds. I was in desperate need of transformation and it was the Lord Himself who was giving me insight in my mind of how to put His Word into practice. I knew I could not continue to dwell upon the negative if I was to climb out of the funk I was in. Then the Holy Spirit whispered for me to tear the complaint and grateful words paper in half, and be done with the complaining. I threw the negativity in the trash and committed the list to the Lord. I was to daily thank God out loud for all the things I was grateful for and to add to the list as I became aware of more. This exercise helped me to begin to change my behavior and press more into Jesus as He was renewing my mind and healing my heart.

As I drew closer to Him, He began to talk to me about these new irrational fears I was carrying. I asked the Lord to deliver me from them and to help me face each one. A favorite promise of God is that when you ask, you shall receive. When you seek, you shall find. When you ask of God, in a way that shows you are completely at His mercy, and depending on Him to show up on your behalf, He hears and answers. I was desperate for deliverance and I was asking for help! But again, His answer requires a response of faith as the remedy involves obedience. Remember? Faith moves! Faith is an action command. The Word does not say we sit in faith, but rather we walk by faith, not by sight and we walk in faith, not in fear.

Perhaps you've heard the saying that F.E.A.R. is False Expectations Appearing Real. To get over your fear, you must face your fears head on by faith and see for yourself that what you had feared did not come to pass but is now a thing in your past. This is the only way to internalize and own the belief that you are truly free from your fears, when you allow the Holy Spirit to guide your faith steps toward freedom. Each faith step unlocks the next step and before you realize it, you forget what you had been afraid of because you become aware you are no longer afraid. Faith in God frees us from ALL fear!

Fear was forced to flee . . .

Through intercessory prayer from others on my behalf and my heart desiring to be free, the "spirit of fear" left the building, and I felt it leave my body when it did. A dear friend was silently praying for me in my room while I rested. I can't explain it but I was aware of it when fear was ejected from my body. I was free! I called upon the Lord and He heard my cry. He answered me in my time of need. He delivered me from evil and from the evil spirit of fear. He came to my rescue and put courage and faith deep inside my core. The gift of friends who stand in the gap and intercede on behalf of their friends is a priceless treasure. I'm grateful for Celia.

With new courage, I began to face each fear one by one and through the power of the Holy Spirit, Jesus and I together overcame them all. My healing was being released in my mind, and as a result, my body was returning to normal as well. There is much I am leaving out purposefully but I want you to comprehend that there is nothing we face that our Lord does not understand. We have no hurts He cannot heal, and by His stripes, Jesus has already paid the price for our healing in our body, our spirit and in our soul. We are not left alone or abandoned and we are not expected to remain in bondage to the grave clothes we had been wearing when the Lord set us free.

The devil is a liar! Fear is a liar! Our God is able to deliver us from all fear, evil and all strongholds but we must put our hope, faith and trust in Him! And we must act on our faith with whatever faith we have and walk out of the grave into new life with Christ. If you need more faith, call upon the name of Jesus and you will be saved and will receive a new measure of faith! You will be saved from yourself, your enemy and the destructive path you are walking on. He will be your ever-present help in your time of trouble. His faithful promises are true and will be your shield and rampart. It is a promise of God—a promise received by faith. His faithful mercies are fresh every day. Joy comes in the morning and melts our mourning into new mercies and sparks new joy into our day, every day! Hallelujah! I am a living testimony of this truth!

The Word does not say we sit in faith, but rather we walk by faith, not by sight and we walk in faith, not in fear.

CHAPTER 8

HEALED BY THE WORD

In a nutshell, I disclosed to Pastor Ron all these personal matters I've just shared with you. I was confused that I had suffered from these mental moments even though I had forgiven everyone, was living for Jesus and seemed to be doing well most of the time. I had noticed that the previous three occurrences had happened when I had experienced grief, fatigue and a spiritual high all within a short period prior to the physiological crash. I had believed perhaps grief was always the trigger but I had not experienced grief this last time, to my knowledge. Pastor Ron agreed there was some truth to what I had perceived in some ways, but that I was not to agree with that diagnosis as it does not have to happen every time grief pops up and there were other factors we needed to address.

I had indeed finished the grieving cycle a number of years ago prior, regarding the premature death of my mom and baby sister. But there was a new prolonged process of grief lingering in the air as Greg's father was hanging on for his life in and out of hospice. I'll explain.

The trends of trauma - I see a pattern . . .

As I processed the episodes from the past, I acknowledged to Ron that grief and fear of personal loss, after a close friend passed away, had played into my second episode about ten years ago. And then the summer of 2019, I had several traumatic things happen at once. A wild animal killed our dog Chloe, when she got out of the yard undetected on my watch. Just a few days prior, I had a devastating and disturbing conversation happen between me and someone close to me which has since been resolved and forgiven, but at the time was painful in my heart. During this time, our middle daughter moved to another state as she had graduated college and was beginning a new journey. Just a month prior to Chloe's death, I pre-planned my father-in-law's funeral as the family was told he was going to die within a few days. He lived another eight months, with Lewy Body Dementia, but I still grieved the loss when I pre-planned his funeral, complete with videos, the program, and details arranged for full military honors.

It was emotional and painful to go through all of this at once. At the same time, I was an event organizer for a non-profit pregnancy clinic and was planning a huge event that was carried out the day before Chloe got out. My husband and I had also just participated in an intercessory prayer event a few weeks before we were told we were losing his dad. An emotional train was speeding up and approaching a dangerous intersection in my mind. I was grieving, exhausted, excited, overwhelmed, hurting and confused and had experienced a spiritual high all within a short period of time. I felt the weight of much responsibility on my shoulders and those who know me well know that when I take on a responsibility, I like to do it well or not at all. I have a habit of putting undue pressure on myself to go above and beyond what is expected because I truly like to do things with excellence and enjoy the process.

The weight of everything took a toll on me and I took a mental dive, but God miraculously pulled me through it in a few short days. This third episode occurred just over six months prior to this last and final occurrence, as I am declaring it done by faith. I believe this to be true as in retrospect, I can see clearly that not only was my body in hyperdrive for the months in between, but I now know there were some deep inner beliefs and strongholds that I needed to be delivered from. I did not know this before my deliverance Zoom session with Pastor Ron Frizzel in the spring of 2020. But the power of the Holy Spirit revealed things to him and I confirmed it as we took a walk down memory lane in route to stepping onto the path of freedom.

Remembering and acknowledging can be somewhat painful but God never wastes a pain. He uses the pressure of pain to produce a pearl in your heart. He makes beauty from ashes as He heals and He restores your soul in the process. Vocalizing the part of my testimony I never wanted to admit to was making me feel lighter and was freeing my spirit. I kept talking and Ron dug deeper into my past, clear back to my first breath. "Let's talk about your mom," he said.

Mom, what were you thinking? . . .

It saddened my heart to think about some of the pain my mother must have carried in hers as I thought through some of what she perhaps experienced. Though she had a loving family, it was a blended one and they were not perfect as none of us are. She married right out of High School and became pregnant soon after while my dad went to ministry school. My parents moved states, as my dad became a pastor straight out of college. It was a tiny Kansas church that was not able to pay much, but their needs were met. The pressures of a pastor's family are great and learning to be a wife, a mom and a pastor's wife all at once, away from her family, I'm sure was a difficult thing to do. My mom was a fun loving mom and took great care of her family, as did my dad. But sometimes I remember during my early teenage years, she would talk about wanting to go to heaven in a way I do not yet desire to go at this time of my life. I want to go when my time is right, and I look forward to spending eternity with Jesus and loved ones, but I am not looking to escape and go now. Looking back I wonder if she was suffering from a form of depression. I do not know. She was so young, as was I, and I am left with many questions.

Mom worked hard and did her part to help with the family finances. She was also very creative and resourceful, which I picked up from her and my dad. She used to make gifts, plan a party on a dime, cook delicious but inexpensive meals, dream up fun cheap things to do as a family, and make sure we knew how much Jesus loved us. Sometimes, I wish I could visit with her and find out more about her life, her childhood, her experiences and her feelings. I was fourteen when she went to live with Jesus, so I can only go on what I remember, knowing there is much I do not know. I can say this, that she had compassion for others, truly cared about people and loved her family and God with all her heart. I do not know what she was thinking and feeling when she carried me, but given what I do know, I'm sure it was not easy.

You are what you think . . .

On a side note, I have learned much about how our DNA is altered by what we think and feel which is then passed down to our offspring. Do you realize we can alter our own DNA by the renewing of our mind and by changing our habits, attitudes, beliefs and behaviors? We can turn unhealthy cells to healthy ones and we can rewire our brains by the renewing of our minds, therefore creating healthier DNA. This is true for future passing of healthy DNA and it is also true of receiving health to DNA that was received from our parents regardless of the nature it was upon conception.

Dr. Caroline Leaf, a Christian neuroscientist, researcher, author, and speaker is to be credited for this information. Look her up on YouTube and read her books. She explains the science that supports the Word of God and teaches you how to put into practice the method to bring health to your decaying brain and health back to your body. The Word of God brings healing down to the marrow and it begins in the mind. We have to reject the enemy's thoughts and fix our thoughts on what the Word of God speaks over us, which is a better word. Within 28 days of agreeing with truth about oneself, the truth takes hold and reverses the curses that had taken root in the mind. The roots are released into His hands and the truth releases healthy cells to take their place. There is overwhelming scientific evidence that supports the promises of God, with pictures included. I love that! Check it out for yourself.

After reflecting upon Mom's life with Pastor Ron, I realized that

I may have received some faulty DNA based on her thoughts and experiences, and I may have also carried some of her beliefs regarding the life of a pastor's family into my spirit. I know I also received a lot of awesome DNA from my parents and I'm not one to hold to the belief that everything wrong is someone else's fault so please don't get me wrong. I do however, understand that a person accepts labels, beliefs, lies and truths and marries them so to speak, then passes them on to the children by way of behavior, words, and altered DNA. As I keep saying, knowledge brings responsibility with it, so with this new insight and consideration, I repented of the possibility I had been operating in false beliefs and I asked the Lord for another layer of deliverance. I chose His better Word instead of hanging onto mine. His ways are higher than ours but He was sharing His thoughts with me. I was being set free and I felt it! Freedom feels good!

A preacher's kid perspective . . .

Until you've been there, you don't know what it's like, and growing up a preacher's kid, I have some insight into what pastors and their wives go through. When I was a child, our churches that my dad pastored always provided a house, we referred to as a parsonage. It was wonderful in that we had a provided home to live in, but my mom was never able to paint, remodel or feel like it was hers. Although grateful for the home, I do remember her being upset that my dad had to get church board approval for her to paint our house and it was sometimes denied. As a wife and one who loves to decorate my own home, I can imagine the frustration she must've felt at times. She was always rearranging our furniture in our home, and as I think of it, it was probably because it was the only thing she could do to get a new look. It makes perfect sense to me now. As always, Mom somehow made a way and she found a way to have fun doing it. I do not remember my parents arguing or raising their voices in front of us kids. I know they like all couples had conflict, but they worked through it and modeled love to the family. That being said, I am also not aware of what was going on in her heart. When I was at the age I was interested in relating to her on a deeper level, she was gone. Many of my recollections shared with

Ron were based on speculation and the memories I could recall.

My dad has always been compassionate and has been a great pastor everywhere he has served. I am grateful for my friendship with him and the belief that he poured into my life encouraging me to go after my dreams and not settle for less. But I do remember as a young child that there were often times that our plans got changed due to a family in the church who was in need, or a responsibility he had at the church. Dad often had church events he had to attend which kept him from attending some family plans. He was, as I am, dedicated to everything he says he will do, and as a pastor of a smaller church, many responsibilities fall on you. Recalling memories from a child's point of view, these times may not have happened as often as I remember, but in my young mind, I managed to form the belief system that the church always came first. I did not realize this until recently, but I can see throughout my life that it indeed has stuck with me and shaped many of my behaviors.

While I was in college, I always asked the boys I was interested in what their major was, and if it was religion, I took my cue and lost interest immediately. I did not want to keep living the lifestyle I was accustomed to, though my home was a loving home. I developed the belief that the "perception" of the pastor's family was of "utmost" importance. The testimony and reputation of the pastor was determined by the behavior of his family, so I thought, and it was to be guarded and protected at all costs. This again, was not spoken to me but was a belief system I adapted due to behaviors I witnessed and things perceived. The way others considered my dad was a big deal and important to the ministry. This was a false belief system, but it was my belief system because of my perception. Though it wasn't true, it contributed to the way I thought and felt about people in ministry. Pastor Ron helped me to see that through this belief system, I had held onto the wounds of it and made judgments based on it, so on behalf of preachers, he repented and asked me to forgive him. A first! I didn't see that coming. I received it with tears in my eyes and in his, as I felt the love of the Father coming through this anointed man of God. I felt freedom return to my body. The anointing breaks the heavy yoke and sets us free.

A little girl no more . . .

You don't forget some things but you may forget about them so you can move on. I had forgotten about some experiences I had as a little girl that put adult thoughts and fears into my innocent mind. Pastor Ron heard stories of how I escaped being molested by teenage boys in our church who had made sexual attempts at me when I was in the second grade. I did not confess these things to my parents at the time because the boys were from families my parents were friends with and I was afraid to talk about it. Years later after I was married, I revealed the stories to my dad. I had felt dirty as a young girl, that I had done something wrong and that I needed to protect my dad's reputation, after all, because he was the pastor. Two different boys on two different occasions educated me sexually and made advances that I by the grace of God was able to divert. I didn't understand what was going on, but I knew it wasn't right and I was spared, thanks be to God. This was when I first started believing that boys could not be trusted. I had a few other private experiences as a teenager that fueled the belief. Though I managed to escape each time, each one added a layer to the deep-seeded belief system I was forming in my mind.

Eyes to see . . .

Pastor Ron allowed me to see that I had been held bondage to these beliefs and had never really allowed the Lord to heal my mind in these areas. In fact, because I had agreed with the false assessments for so long, every time I learned of men or ministry leaders who had messed up, I was not surprised and the deep-rooted belief continued to grow. Ron humbly stood in the gap for people in ministry and for men in general, as again, with tears in his eyes, he asked me to forgive him for hurting me. I had never had anyone do this before, as a substitute, to give me a tangible person to forgive on behalf of another. We both were in tears as I released men and ministry leaders from the grip I had held in my mind and deep in my heart for so long. Bitterness is the word we often refer to as unforgiveness, and as I stated before, its presence prevents our healing. It creates a roadblock in our hearts and minds that keeps us from getting through the traps the enemy lays for us. But when we become aware, and allow the Lord to remove them, we are free to live, love and hope again.

I am so very grateful for God's timing and even for the painful process it took for me to be delivered. The Lord knows the number of our days, and just fourteen days before Pastor Ron Frizzell stepped into eternity, God allowed our intersection in a Zoom Room to take place. He guided me through remembrance and then through deliverance prayers and gave me insight that will take me through the rest of my life. I have peace in my heart and I am so grateful for this man of God. One day, I will get to hug his neck and meet him in person in heaven and properly thank him for sacrificing his time to allow the Lord to heal me through his ministry. The effects will be duplicated, as I will carry it on to others and have begun with the words you are reading.

With a Pure heart & mind - came insight to thrive . . .

The visit with Ron was two months prior to meeting Rev. Jay Jellison, so by the time I met Jay, my heart had been delivered and purified and I was no longer in bondage. I learned how to care for my body so I would not enter into another enemy trap. The tools the Lord sent me when I wasn't looking are not only for me but I hope they are tools you can use to receive your healing. Perhaps it is not for you but someone you know who needs to hear this story. It's good to know you're not alone and there is hope for your healing on the horizon.

When we take care of our spiritual issues first, our bodies will often line up and respond as well. It is crazy how many things we suffer in our body that are tied to a belief, a bond, an unforgiving spirit, a generational curse, or grief or trauma not yet dealt with. Don't get me wrong. I do believe in taking care of the body, seeing a doctor when necessary, taking proper medications, eating well, getting a good night's sleep and exercising. I have received healing through these means as well as a touch of Jesus during a prayer of faith and with the laying on of hands. I am now gaining understanding that physical healing also comes to us through repentance, deliverance and forgiveness.

God is so gentle and patient with us, and the Holy Spirit is the best teacher! Thank you, Jesus, for making it possible to live in freedom as we wait with expectation for the day we are transformed and receive our eternal reward. But until that day, I choose to live a life fully devoted to Christ and to walking in the authority and freedom He paid for me to enjoy. The son set me free and I am free indeed! I am compelled to share Christ with others and to let His love and light shine through my life. He is more than enough to satisfy me. Great is His faithfulness. His mercies are fresh and new every day!

Treasure found in the midst of trauma . . .

Though trauma and grief deposited hurt and pain, the process and journey to healing has produced good in my life. Through the grief, the fruit of joy has emerged. Through the trauma, the fruit of peace has settled on me. Through the disappointments, the fruit of faithfulness has flourished. Through the trials, the fruit of love has been the harvest and kindness, gentleness and goodness has certainly followed me. What the enemy has meant to destroy me with has instead become my testimony. I will forever treasure the relationship I have with Jesus for all He has done to heal my heart and mind while working through the trauma in my life. He has been closer than a brother to me and He is my greatest treasure. In the midst of trauma, I found priceless treasure!

Good grief, I'm healed! . . .

I am an overcomer by the blood of the lamb, the word of my testimony and that I am not afraid of losing my life. My life is in His hands and I will live out all the days He has ordained for me. I am a daughter of the Most High God, and I am in love with Jesus! The devil did not give me peace and he cannot take it away. The peace I possess is the peace that surpasses all my understanding. I've been hurt in the world, which has brought me much grief, but I've been healed by the Word, which has in turn, set me free. What started out bad has turned for my good. God is good. The healing grief process has produced an unexpected joy in the "mourning" as His mercies are fresh and new each "morning." God has indeed turned my grief into good and now I am free! Good grief! I'm healed! My grief has turned into peace and the Word of God has rooted it deep in my heart and mind. Jesus said, *"I am leaving you with a gift—peace of mind and heart. And the peace I give is a gift the world cannot give. So don't be troubled or afraid." John 14:27 NLT*

To live a peaceful and happy life, we must live a forgiven life. To live forgiven, we must forgive. This is a life of total transparency and one of trusting in the Lord moment by moment. This walk of forgiveness is a walk in His abiding presence. It is a place of safety, security and sweet communion with our risen Savior. I cannot think of any other place I'd rather be. Soak in His love and pause in His presence.

I woke up this morning hearing Psalms 32 in my spirit. The Passion Translation stuck out to me like a love letter from the Lord and I knew it was how I was to bring this section to a close. May this beautiful Word of God bring peace to your soul and healing to your mind by the power of the living and active voice of the Holy Spirit in each word.

A Poem of Insight by King David, from The Passion Translation: "Forgiven"

"I hear the Lord saying, "I will stay close to you, instructing and guiding you along the pathway for your life. I will advise you along the way and lead you forth with my eyes as your guide. So don't make it difficult; don't be stubborn when I take you where you've not been before. Don't make Me tug you and pull you along. Just come with Me!" How happy and fulfilled are those whose rebellion has been forgiven, those whose sins are covered by blood. How blessed and relieved are those who have confessed their corruption to God! For He wipes their slates clean and removes hypocrisy from their hearts. Before I confessed my sins, I kept it all inside; my dishonesty devastated my inner life, causing my life to be filled with frustration, irrepressible anguish, and misery. The pain never let up, for Your hand of conviction was heavy on my heart. My strength was sapped, my inner life dried up like a spiritual drought within my soul. Pause in His presence! Then I finally admitted to You all my sins, refusing to hide them any longer. I said,

"My life-giving God, I will openly acknowledge my evil actions." And You forgave me! All at once the guilt of my sin washed away and all my pain disappeared! Pause in His presence! This is what I've learned through it all: All believers should confess their sins to God; do it every time God has uncovered you in the time of exposing. For if you do this, when sudden storms of life overwhelm, you'll be kept safe. Lord, you are my secret hiding place, protecting me from these troubles, surrounding me with songs of gladness! Your joyous shouts of rescue release my breakthrough. Pause in His presence! So, my conclusion is this: Many are the sorrows and frustrations of those who don't come clean with God. But when you trust in the Lord for forgiveness, His wrap-around love will surround you. So celebrate the goodness of God! He shows this kindness to everyone who is His. Go ahead—shout for joy, all you upright ones who want to please Him!" Psalms 32:1-11 TPT (Reference the Resources at the end of the book for a beautiful video message based on Psalms 32, titled: "Surrounded by Mercy.")

Though trauma and grief deposited hurt and pain, the process and journey to healing has produced good in my life.

SECTION TWO

REMAIN IN THE WORD
~
MAINTAIN THE HEALING!

CHAPTER 9

ROOTED AND ESTABLISHED

My Prayer:

Father God, thank you for your gift of salvation, for your presence, your healing touch, and for your Word! Your Word is nourishment to my soul and is my daily bread! You have taken my brokenness and hurts I've received in this world, and by your Word, I have been healed! Lord, open up the eyes and ears of your people so we all may receive healing and walk in freedom with you. Root us in your love and establish us in a life of prayer and communion with your Word. I love you! Suzanne

Extract those garden weeds out by the root! If you don't, the weeds will grow back, the roots will go deeper, will take over and become harder to handle. This is a metaphor of what takes place in our hearts when we don't deal with the root, or source of our issues, as they come up. Instead, we water the emotional roots as we dwell upon them, become angry and keep them fresh and alive. We hold onto bitterness and talk constantly about the festering roots. Before long, we find our focus is on the weeds we see popping up but forget we have catered to the roots for a very long time, and in doing so, we have inadvertently preserved them. Over time, we completely forget about the source of the root or the acknowledgment of its existence. We think we behave or think "this way" because it's just "who we are" when in fact we have a "mistaken sense of our own identity." We just know we get emotional or upset when the irritating weeds keep surfing but we don't even know why.

It's essential that you identify the root source of your emotional wound and the place where open doors for the enemy to walk through have been made. It takes work to figure it out but it is helpful if you can find a professional Christian counselor or a minister who practices and specializes in deliverance ministry, who can walk you through the process of getting to the root cause. It may be painful and you may be surprised at what you find. It will be tempting to discount what is revealed to you because you don't want to believe that either you had developed a faulty mindset, or that you had experienced a trauma or unresolved grief that your mind had hidden from you. When you get a new revelation, you will be taken back to moments in time in which you will have to acknowledge things you had no knowledge of or had forgotten about. In order for you to forgive from the deepest places of your heart, you have to be willing to open up your heart to allow the Lord to reveal to your mind what He wants to, in order to heal you.

Again, you may already be walking with the Lord and trusting Him as your savior, but still have deep inner healing that you have not yet received. Jesus cares about all of you and He says in His living active Word, that He came not only to give us life, but an exceedingly abundant life, greater than our wildest imaginations. An abundant, full, restored life is waiting to be shared when we come to the feet of Jesus with open arms and a desire to be made whole. The Holy Spirit fills the believer to capacity but if a section of your heart houses bitterness, fear or something else you won't let go of, your available space for the Holy Spirit to dwell in, becomes limited. When you clean the house in your heart, which He will do in you if you want Him to, then you make room for Jesus to fill you to capacity with the fullness of His

Spirit. Is there room in your Inn for Him?

He wants to heal your heart and mind but there may be a door that is closed to Jesus at this time. He stands at the door of your heart and knocks. Will you let Him in so He can help locate the other doors that need to be opened to Him for healing or to be closed to the enemy to evacuate hidden darkness?

The open door …

You can't close a door unless you know where it exists and how it got opened. Jesus knows where the doors are and the Holy Spirit will guide the process of locating them, when asked. These doors have most likely been opened because of agreements made with lies believed regarding your past, your mindsets and perspectives that are not in alignment with your true identity in Christ. Sneaky traps get laid for believers to fall into which open the doors for opportunity to hit you out of nowhere at a later unexpected time in your life. These doors, when opened, allow fear to surface and it shows up in a variety of forms such as anxiety, panic attacks, feelings of abandonment, rejection, confusion and perhaps a lack of personal value.

The Holy Spirit may reveal a deeper level of understanding to you in order to heal your heart and break off generational bonds that have kept you captive to them. Consider these questions you might ask of Him:

Ask the Holy Spirit to reveal to you what doors have not been closed that need to be.

Ask the Holy Spirit what has been partnered with that needs to be dissolved.

Ask the Holy Spirit to renew any mindset and perspective you believe that is an open door to fear. We do not want to give the devil a window of opportunity or a door to devour. We must receive a new mindset from Christ to replace the old one we've let go of. We get a change of ownership in our minds when we do.

I am not what I do or what I did …

The enemy has attacked my identity in the past with confusion, causing me to believe that my identity is anything but that as a child of God. However, my true identity is seated and rooted in Christ alone. I am a child of God, a righteous, holy, redeemed, pure, purchased, created, cleansed, forgiven daughter of the Most High God because I'm in Jesus Christ, and He is in me. I have this deposit of the Holy Spirit in my heart as a gift I received from Jesus when I accepted Him as my savior and surrendered my life to Him. The presence of God continuously fills me with joy, occupies me with hope and is my overflowing life-giving Living Water! No wonder the attacks come after our "right standing in Christ" as a son or daughter of God. If we don't know "whose" we are, we won't know "who" we are and we will become confused, thinking who we are is "what we do." As a result, if not careful, we buy into the lies of the need for striving, performance, idolatry and pride as we bind our identity to these false gods while grieving God's heart.

I bet you can relate in some way as the devil is not creative and he comes at us all in similar ways. He has lied and has tried to convince me my identity is in my abilities or what has been done to me, or in who I know or what people think of me. He has absolutely messed with my mind when I've dwelled on sinful desires, and I hold him responsible for trying to rob me of joy, relationships and dreams, which he has at times accomplished for a short time. The plans the enemy has for a Christ follower is this: to kill, to steal and to destroy. Period. I have personally had family members killed and my marriage was nearly murdered; money and dreams have been stolen; and I've had relationships and plans destroyed... how about you? BUT GOD!

The Lord is faithful and because Jesus Christ is King, His plans ALWAYS prevail. The plans God has for a Christ follower is this: He gives life and He heals; He restores and returns what was stolen; and He makes ALL things new. Jesus destroys the works of the devil and we get to participate when we walk by faith and trust the promises of God and in hearing the voice of the Holy Spirit. Our value and worth is determined by our identity in Christ alone and in Him, we are priceless!

Because we find our identity as sons and daughters of the Most High God, we are destined for eternity and are wired for love. It is important we do not get our identity and destiny out of order or we will lose our identity in the process. We must not let that happen. We are rooted in love as a beloved child of God and that beautiful identity determines our destiny, which is eternity in heaven!

I am confident of this …

Jesus has healed my marriage and has saved my family; He has restored finances that the enemy stole, and though my mom and sister's lives were taken from this earth, they stepped right into eternity safe in the arms of Jesus forever. *2 Corinthians 5:8* NKJV reminds us that *"to be absent from the body is to be present with the Lord,"* and I take courage in knowing that when mom and Jennifer took their last breaths on earth, they were breathing their first breaths in heaven's atmosphere, in the presence of God. In Christ, there is true freedom, abundant life and hope for eternity and there is no existence of death, evil or fear!

The only thing that can be killed is the physical body as our spirit man lives forever, for those who are in Christ Jesus. The enemy cannot take, kill, or destroy my spirit, hope, joy, peace or my identity in Christ! However, he has inflicted deep wounds upon me. There are events in my life that have been traumatizing to me that have left impressions in my subconscious. These impressions have had an impact on many things that I do, think, and say. Out of hurt, confusion, fear and the need to survive, behaviors have been formed. And as I've recently been reminded, the subconscious mind takes over and we may not even realize the deep thoughts of our hearts that have shaped our attitude and behaviors.

The emotional water table…

Emotions are formed as an equal and opposite reaction to events that take place in your life. But for reasons affected by past memories, family atmospheres or generational inheritance, emotions of a wounded heart, are often suppressed and stuffed deep into the spirit. They are not permitted to surface, as a means of self-survival or in attempt to protect another. This act is not something we necessarily are conscious of but nonetheless, it happens. Without realizing it, a habit is formed and anytime a similar event in life occurs, the emotion is added to the previous one. It adds another layer, further deepening the wound and lengthening the root while burying it further into the spirit.

According to Ron, the emotional water table buried deep below the surface of our consciousness is also watered every time we add another layer of emotion to it. We continue to water it and because we've not dealt with it, there comes a point where it surfaces when we least expect it and it deals with us, most often as an unexpected surprise. We shouldn't prevent these emotions from coming to the surface, in order to deal with them as they arise. If we try to "do something" to hide our emotions instead of "dealing with them," our doing only causes us to cover them up further and bury them deeper, until they surface later and deal with you.

In my case, fear had been suppressed! For almost 30 years, I'd dealt with fear on many levels. I have been delivered from the spirit of fear and no longer walk with it or abide in it. The wounds and scars fear left had however, submerged in my spirit at an unconscious level had been left alone and not dealt with. I was in need of healing at a very deep level within my spirit. Jesus taught us to pray like this, "Our Father who art in Heaven...deliver us from evil..." The Holy Spirit worked through Pastor Ron to answer this prayer in my life. Fear is of the enemy. Fear is a liar! Praise God I have been delivered from the dwelling presence of the evil of fear and of the fear of evil.

In His Image: Body, Soul, Spirit, and Will ...

We are wonderfully made in the image of God and we are made with a body, spirit, and soul. Although our physical body, or tent, is flesh and blood, it is also a temporary Temple of God, which houses our unseen spirit and soul. We are to care for it and trust God as we live in it. God knitted our spirit together with our body inside our mother's womb. Our soul is what Jesus saved from spiritual death by His sacrificial blood, through His resurrection and ascension back to the Father. The enemy hates our souls but cannot snatch us from God, although he tries his best to hurt Jesus by tricking us into believing lies and agreeing with him. He tirelessly works to cause pain to the body of Christ because he wants to hurt Jesus and the heart of God by doing so. Be aware it has never been about me and it has never been about you. It is all about Jesus!

Our soul, housed in our mind's heart, is our personality, our gifting's, our unique identifiers and it is relational. The health of the soul determines the health of the heart. When we hang onto offense and hurts, though our soul is not damaged (because it is safe with Jesus when we believe and receive the gift of salvation), our spirit has absorbed the pain, and it is in need of receiving inner healing to receive freedom to release health back to our body.

Our spirit is made up of our mind, our will, and our emotions. Our inward spirit manifests outward behaviors, which affects our overall wellbeing. Our conscious mind thinks and reasons and is the place of our awareness. Our subconscious mind, however, is where we form our beliefs, attitudes, feelings and emotions. It is also where our long-term memories are tucked, buried and placed in a mental storage unit.

Our will is what we activate to make choices for our body. Personal choices affect inner nerves as well as the immune system, and it motivates outward actions. What we think and believe in our mind affects our overall physical health! Not only are we what we eat; we are what we think. *Proverbs 23:7 NKJV* tells us *"For as he thinks in his heart, so is he."*

A change of citizenship...

Here's the thing: sin is present so we are affected by it because we live in a sinful world. But Christ has overcome the world and those who are in Him, are new creations. When we who are in Jesus Christ, receive Him, we instantly move our spiritual eternal citizenship to heaven and we suddenly begin to live as foreigners in the world. Foreigners have a choice when they choose to live or are forced to live in a land that is not of their own culture. They can choose to abandon their culture and live as a citizen in the land they reside in, or they can adapt to the culture where they live while maintaining their citizenship / native culture and community. As children of God, we are in the world but not of it, so we are not to conform to the patterns of the world, but to be transformed by the renewing of our minds. We are to live as the influencers for Jesus, as Christ's ambassadors, while living as temporary residents in the world. Salt is tasty and beneficial. Light breaks the darkness and is helpful to those around. This is how we influence: by "being" the salt and light so the Holy Spirit can "do" the greater works through our love and obedience to Christ and His Word. It is a simply beautiful way to live our lives peacefully as citizens of Heaven, seeded and seated (rooted and established) in heavenly places hidden in Christ, while wearing shoes of gospel peace, standing firmly on the ground.

Salt, Light, Value, and Love …

As Christians, we are called to add salt, light, value and love to this world we live in, while understanding we are not of it. We must abide and remain in the light and love of God so we can emit and reflect what we've absorbed onto others. It is also essential to our health and to the health of our fellow believers that we remain in community with the body of Christ. *Hebrews 10:25 ESV* reminds us to *"not neglect meeting together, as is the habit of some, but encourage one another, and all the more as you see the day drawing near."*

We are to do as the early believers did and stay true to the teachings of the Word of the gospel; we are to be in koinonia Christian fellowship with our small tribe of believers whom we trust to be real and vulnerable with. We are also to eat and take communion together and we are to pray together and for one another. But in order to come into this physical place of koinonia, we must be in a proper spiritual place, ourselves. To bring to the community what we have to offer that will benefit and add value to the community, we must have our own spiritual priorities in order and come from a place of healing, wholeness, and fullness.

Seek first…

Before we seek advice, opinions, confirmation, or validation from others, we must first seek the Kingdom of God and His righteousness, then He will add it to our lives, as we find in *Matthew 6:33*. Everything else will fall into place at the right time as added benefits when we follow the two new commandments Jesus gave us. First, we must love the Lord Our God with all our heart, soul, mind and strength. And second, we must love our neighbor, or others, as we love ourselves. If we do not truly love ourselves as a complete, whole, healthy and healed son or daughter of God, identified by Christ Jesus in us - we cannot truly love others the way Christ intends for us to love.

We must allow Jesus, by the help of the Holy Spirit, to take us to new depths of rooted distress we've submerged at a level we were unaware existed in our innermost being. It is this intimate place of our hearts Jesus intends to attend to.

Jesus is the vine in the Tree of Life and His Father, our Father, is the gardener. When there are roots that produce bad fruit or don't produce fruit at all, the whole tree is affected. The roots that are not rooted in the vine of Jesus, become weeds and hindrances to the health of the branches, causing the whole tree to suffer. These fruitless branches have to be removed. They must be pruned from the branch at the root or they will spring up again and damage the harvest.

Breaking FREE …

Spiritually speaking, Jesus said we must be transformed by the renewing of our minds. If He didn't mean it, He wouldn't have said it. If not possible, Jesus wouldn't have presented the process in which we could be made new. Transformation takes place after we renew our minds, not before. Ask the Lord to reveal to you what He wants to transform in you. Ask God to renew your mind at the subconscious level where the triggers of emotion are stimulated.

To renew our mind, including our set of beliefs, our feelings and emotions, which determine our actions, we must choose to perceive differently. We must respond to the new revelation. Forsake a former thought and embrace a new thought, or rather, repent and turn from the way we were going, doing our own thing, and return to God, and follow His ways.

Even though the subconscious mind houses these things we've submerged through stuffing, denying and not dealing with, there is hope for healing in our innermost being. Not only do we have a responsibility to change the way we believe by what we choose to think upon, but we also have a responsibility to respond to the work of the Holy Spirit who will reveal things to us so God can restore and renew our spirit.

If you feel overwhelmed by many emotions surfacing all at once, as the Holy Spirit brings them to your mind, make sure if you are not already in the care of a professional grief counselor, to seek help. Please do not stuff your emotions or assume they will go away on their own. If you, however, receive one or two things to your remembrance and you work through them by allowing the Lord to heal you, and you feel lighter in your spirit because of it, you may not need a professional counselor. I have personally benefited at different times from the help of a professional. There have been other times I have contacted a trusted friend or advisor who is led by the Holy Spirit and has given me a safe place to confess and share my heart, and receive godly wisdom or advice. Sometimes, when the Holy Spirit reveals something new to me, I find relief by writing in my prayer journal, praying, reading my Bible and then confessing to someone so I may be healed.

We have not because we ask not...

When we ask God with pure and right motives to reveal to our minds the areas He wishes to heal and restore, He will answer. If we do not ask of Him to receive this inner healing, we most likely will not receive it. He wants to heal. In the Bible we read time after time, before Jesus healed someone, He asked, "What do you want?" Then He required them to do something by faith in participation with the healing He was imparting to them. Sometimes, the requirement was to go dip in dirty water, or it was as simple as getting up and walking. The healing always required a personal <u>desire</u> to receive it, a <u>request</u> for it and a <u>response</u> to Jesus by doing what He said, by acting on it in faith.

How about you? Do you want to be healed? If you do, ask Him to reveal things so you may repent of wrong behaviors, beliefs and mindsets that have held you captive. Break the ties that have tethered you to the things that have hindered you from walking in ultimate true freedom. Replace those former thoughts by declaring with your voice in agreement who Jesus Christ is, as the redeeming Son of God and the only way to receive eternal life. Testify to your own soul and to another person of your acknowledgment of what Jesus has done for you through His death on the cross and His resurrection to life. Receive the fire, power and fullness of the Holy Spirit as a gift from God to help you live and dwell in Him while living a full and free life in expectation of Christ's return. And finally, ASK Jesus to cleanse, purify and completely heal and restore your heart and mind, thereby making you a new creation.

Remember, Jesus bought your salvation, your healing and your freedom with His very life, then He poured out His Spirit into the believer's hearts after He ascended back to the Father and took His seat next to Him, declaring victory over the devil and over death. So, as purified, cleansed, healed sons and daughters of God, we now have this confident assurance in Christ. Now that we KNOW we have received Christ, and now that we KNOW Him intimately, we KNOW we can, by faith, believe we have been set free. We are free to get up & walk! And by all means, we must tell somebody! As we take that step by an act of faith, we receive the faith to take the next step.

The Lord is a gentle God and He never forces Himself upon us. He leads us, guides us and speaks to our hearts. Jesus said, "My sheep hear and know My voice." However, we must be listening in order to hear and if we are always busy hustling, our hearing may become impaired. The Lord says for us to *be still and know that He is God.* We also know He doesn't speak to us in the middle of chaos, disorder or confusion. He speaks in a still small voice and when we are still and at rest, we are in sync with His perfect rhythms and we have the ability to listen, hear and discern what the Spirit is saying.

We love to give our children good gifts. How much more our heavenly Father loves to give good gifts to us and will give the Holy Spirit to those who ask. When we are truly healed at our deepest level, we will be housing the full presence of the Lord in our spirit. We will be one in spirit with Jesus Christ according to: *I Corinthians 6:17 NIV,* *"But whoever is united with the Lord is one with him in spirit."* I know this to be true because the Word of God tells me so, and because I have experienced for myself this healing fullness of Christ Himself infused into my spirit, uniting us together. It is Christ who abides in me who is my hope and your hope of future glory! Once you have experienced the abiding presence of the Lord, no one can convince you otherwise. You know that you know that you know in whom you believe because of what you've personally perceived and in what you've received. The Holy Spirit still guides, reveals and teaches us unto all things, just as Jesus said he would do. *Psalms 25:5 NLT reads, "Lead Me by your truth and teach me, for you are the God who saves me. All day long I put my hope in you."* In God I hope and trust!

Transformation takes place after we renew our minds, not before. Ask the Lord to reveal to you what He wants to transform in you.

CHAPTER 10

PRIORITIZE AND EMPHASIZE

My Prayer:

Father God, lead me, teach me, and reveal wrong beliefs I've come into identification with or have buried as a deep-seeded root within my mind and heart. My desire is to remain in your rest, ready to respond to you, God, moment-by-moment and day-by-day. You said to abide in your love and ask what I will and it will be done. I believe in you, and in your faithful promises! May your will be done and my will be gone. I love you! Suzanne

Set things in order with the Lord because everything begins and ends with Jesus Christ. He is the Alpha and the Omega. I have found it is best to seek first the presence of God, then to maintain a healthy temple (or body) in which to carry His presence. When we are living in health and filled with the Holy Spirit, we are prepared to care for and have proper fellowship with our biological and spiritual families and then we are able to carry out effective ministry to others.

Matthew 6:33 NKJV says it best, "But seek first the kingdom of God and his righteousness, and all these things will be added to you."

Thanks to the wisdom of Ron Frizzel, and the help of the Holy Spirit, I have set things in proper order. Here are my four rearranged spiritual realm priorities I have embraced in order to get into and stay in balance physically, to remain in His rest, in His presence and in the will of God. Daily, I must take these priorities to the Lord and trust His leading through them. He is faithful and will do it. He's proven Himself true to me so He will do it again.

Emphasize Spiritual Priorities

Emphasize Spiritual realm priorities to maintain God's order for healing and abiding in His rest:

1. Presence   2. Temple   3. Family   4. Ministry

1. Be aware of His presence daily.

This preeminent presence of Jesus is what I must abide in and be saturated by. It is the ultimate, supreme, unequalled, unrivalled, unsurpassable, incomparable, dominant presence of the Holy Spirit abiding in every cell, every space and in every place in my spirit that makes the difference in everything I depend upon each day. I have chosen to seek His presence first thing every morning because His mercies are new each day, and by seeking Him first, He adds all other things to me and for me. He is my daily bread my body needs to feed upon to receive spiritual nourishment. It's the presence of Christ that I close each day with because I'm grateful for the day I had with Him. His presence actually never leaves my side, but as I become aware of it, it is there where I abide. And as we abide in Him and He in us, we remain in the abiding presence of His rest.

2. Maintain a healthy temple (body) to carry His presence.

My body is the temple the Spirit of God resides in to carry the relationship of His love for me, so I must take care of myself so I may in turn love others. His love saturates me and flows through me to overflow hope to people around me. We are to love our neighbor as ourselves so to love with the Father's love in abundance, we must love ourselves with the love the Father has for us. We care for His Temple when we abide in His perfect love.

Obviously, our complex bodies are made up of flesh, bones, organs, blood, muscles, brains, memories and a whole lot more. They house our souls and our individual spirits so when we receive Jesus as our savior, the heart of God enters and dwells deep within our soul. The mind of Christ dominates the spirit of the believer and Jesus reigns as King of the heart of the redeemed. As a purified and cleansed vessel, the presence of the Holy Spirit is permitted to dwell inside of me and is released to work through me, accomplishing things I could not without Him. This is how we abide in Him! As we are aware we are carrying His presence in our bodies, we should desire to care for the body and treat it with kindness and respect. After all, we are carrying around precious cargo.

The best daily practice we can maintain is to enter into and remain in God's rest. We need His rest to function properly. We must also get physical and mental rest, exercise for our body, and put proper nutrients inside of it. Remember, we are spirit, mind and body and when we are in proper alignment with the Lord, we are one with Him. Our bodies are therefore, His bodies, doing the work of the Father on the earth until He returns to take us home. We are the "bride of Christ" so let's prepare our bodies to meet Him when He calls for us.

Darkness has been evicted …

As I abide in Christ, and He in me, His power works within me. As a result of His presence, I choose daily to evict all darkness from my life by the power vested in me, by the blood of the Lamb of God that runs through my veins. I choose to remain in a state of forgiveness as I've released the pain inflicted upon me in the past by boys and men. I choose to release and relegate the hurt I identified with as a pastor's daughter, believing ministry came before family; and I have embraced the grace that covers a multitude of personal sin, hurts, habits, hang-ups and wrong beliefs.

It's the presence of the Lord that enables me to embrace a new way to live in freedom, without hanging onto the grave clothes I once wore when bound to the old ways of thinking. This girl is done with the rags and now wearing a wedding dress. I am included in the bride of Christ and am anticipating the appearance of our eternal groom.

The death of stress ...

To maintain health, stress must not be permitted to make itself at home in your body. We must destroy stress with intentional rest. Jimmy Winner, M.D says, "Stress isn't just in your head. It's a built-in-physiologic response to a threat. When you're stressed, your body responds. Your blood vessels constrict. Your blood pressure and pulse rise. You breathe faster. Your bloodstream is flooded with hormones such as cortisol and adrenaline. When you're chronically stressed, those physiologic changes, over time, can lead to health problems." Rest allows the Lord to restore you so your health, balance, energy, creativity and sound thinking can return to you.

In Dr. Caroline Leaf's book, *Who Switched off My Brain*, she states: "If you don't build relaxation into your lifestyle you will become a less effective thinker, defeating your ability to accomplish the mental tasks that stole your relaxation in the first place. In fact, for the brain to function like it should, it needs to regroup and consolidate time. If it doesn't get this, it will send out signals in the form of high-level stress hormones, some of which are epinephrine, norepinephrine, and cortisol. If these chemicals constantly flow, they create a "white noise" effect that increases anxiety and blocks clear thinking and the processing of information."

Again, when I have come to a place of total exhaustion and have also experienced great stress or have suffered from traumatic events, the symptoms described by Dr. Jimmy Winner and by Dr. Caroline Leaf has exploded in my body creating havoc, chaos and an inability to hear clearly from the Lord or distinguish reality from the new irrational thoughts that suddenly show up. Science and the medical worlds acknowledge this physical response to be true and they echo the biblical mandate we are given to take rest seriously. The Father's rest has the ability to protect our minds, our bodies and even our souls. God's Word is the best wisdom we have to use as a guide for our health and our hope. *Proverbs 3:7-8 NLT* speaks of this wisdom, *"Don't be impressed with your own wisdom. Instead, fear the Lord and turn away from evil. Then you will have healing for your body and strength for your bones."*

3. Focus on family intimacy

Proper spiritual realm priority within my marriage and with members of my family, begin with intimacy. It is important to enjoy Christian koinonia fellowship with the small group of family members we have been blessed with, and with a small group of friends/believers we do life with. These are the relationships we share in which we have the ability to be real, and not be in fear of being thrown away. These people love you with the love of the Father because they consider you family.

With these in our family and in our family of believers in Jesus that we do this "koinonia fellowship" with, we are to put things in proper order to maintain what was modeled through the early believers. We find the model in *Acts 2:42 NLT, "All the believers devoted themselves to the apostles' teaching, and to fellowship, and to sharing in meals (including the Lord's Supper), and to prayer."*

The Acts 2 format helps to prioritize the family with a spiritual realm mindset:

1. <u>Teach the Word</u> (study it together and live by it)
2. <u>Fellowship</u> with one another (in true koinonia fellowship)
3. <u>Break bread</u> by eating a meal and taking communion together (Keep God as the main focus, remembering the Lord's Supper and the sacrifice of Christ, as opposed to allowing this to become a ritual or common meal.)
4. <u>Prayer</u> - Prayer is out of order if the other things are not operating well and in order. Prayer is powerful but to have agreement with others, which fuels the fire, be in agreement first through the teaching of the Word, fellowship and communion. If you need to forgive someone or ask for personal forgiveness, take care of it first, so you do not block the effectiveness of your prayers.

Please do not enter into a legalistic mindset with this, but be mindful to prioritize the family by doing these things. They will know we are Christians by our love we have for one another. Truly show God's love to each other and draw others to His love by loving one another in this orderly way.

The law of legalism has contributed to the creation of false beliefs that leaves scars, hurts and broken relationships within families and communities. We get bent out of shape over differences of opinion and become offended by the ones we love the most. And equally, we may hurt or offend our closest friends and relatives when we are not in a koinonia fellowship with one another. It is so important that we let go of offense and unite as one in the bond of love because the love bond serves as a guard around those we cherish.

The bonds we hold form strong beliefs as they become rooted deeply within our lives and then are passed down through generations through our DNA and through our behaviors. Let's form the behavior of praying for one another and choosing to care for the needs of each other. Let's pass down the wealth of love, forgiveness, humility and prayerfulness to those who come behind us and to those who live beside us.

True Love wins every time ...

It is important to look beyond the surface level of the way things appear, when quarrels, offense, misunderstandings and hurt feelings take place in the family or in the family of God. One of the enemy's major strategies to destroy us is by causing wicked wedges to be placed between loved ones, including those who love God. We then focus our energies on the situation and details that upset us, and on our own hurting hearts, and we lose focus on Jesus and on the heart of God who is ready to heal and restore.

It is best to take a step back each time this type of attack occurs, and admit to each other that you played a part in fighting with flesh and blood. Acknowledge that enemy plans were behind the misunderstanding and that you are sorry to have participated with them and that you caused hurt or pain. We are clearly told as we have already discussed that our fight is NOT against flesh and blood but rather against the principalities and forces of evil in this dark world. We must call it out, get our armor on, and use our weapons of the Word of God, truth and faith to demolish the stronghold of bitterness. We walk it out when we ask to be forgiven and when we freely forgive, regardless of what created the hurt.

Forgive each other by the grace of the Lord and by the power of the Holy Spirit living within you. Call upon the Lord for help and He will hear you and answer you and He will heal you and help you to forgive others. Again, bond with each other in the bond of love. It is by our love that others will know we follow Christ. It is the love of God witnessed in koinonia fellowship within the family and the believers that attracts others to desire this amazing love of God that He wants to share with them too.

When we choose to forgive and love, and refuse to carry bitterness and offense, people take notice. It is not the world's normal but it is how we live the normal abundant Christian life! Love wins - Every Time!

4. Minister the Father's heart of love from a place of wholeness and rest.

Jesus gave all of His disciples, including us, these two new commandments that when we follow them, will fulfill all the commandments. This is how we minister to others from a place of wholeness and rest. *"And you must love the Lord your God with all your heart, all your soul, all your mind, and all your strength. The second is equally important: 'Love your neighbor as yourself.' No other commandment is greater than these." Mark 12:30-31 NLT*

We have already covered how we can love God with all our heart, soul, mind and strength. As we are loving Him, allowing Jesus to continually cleanse us, heal us, free us and fill us, we will be able to love ourselves as sons and daughters of God, identified with Christ, and filled with the Holy Spirit. Then, we will be able to truly love our neighbors the way God intends for us to do. What a beautiful love He has bestowed upon us so we may also love one another. This is how we minister to others! This is the true ministry of the gospel - loving God and loving others, as we love ourselves. Out of our healed and restored hearts flows the love of God!

You don't know what you don't know, but as soon as you gain awareness of something, you have to choose what you are going to do with it. I truly had thought I had dealt with all fear in my life, but until I met with Ron Frizzell, I was clueless to the deep un-dealt with roots of fear that needed to be dealt with. No wonder I had suffered occasional onsets of mental instability episodes, when my body was at a weak point. I hadn't dealt with fear, so it was dealing with me. I was made aware of scars or impressions that fear had made in my mind. I still needed healing and my mindset and perspective of several things was in need of being renewed in order to permanently close the door to fear in the future. I am grateful the Lord has directed my steps, allowed me to walk through the stages of grief and He has healed my mind. I have been transformed and I have to tell everyone about it because in sharing my testimony of the goodness of God, my faith increases and my hope is that you too will seek to be transformed as well. The journey is not always easy, but the destination makes it worth the trip.

Healed deeply and delivered fully by the Word...

I absolutely love the truth found in *Psalms 139*. It is so intimately personal and represents my desire of how I want to live healed and whole, in a full relationship with the Lord and it sums up everything I've tried to relay so far. God is able to do anything and He does it with excellence. There is nothing He cannot do. He is for you, not against you. He is with you, beside you, within you and all around you. He desires to pour out His favor and blessings upon you and He wants to give you peace. His Word is a light to our path, it is nourishment to our souls and it carries healing to our marrow.

God's Word is the FINAL Word and I will end this chapter with His Word. Feast upon these portions of *Psalms 139* taken from The Passion Translation and be filled to overflowing with glorious hope!

"You are so intimately aware of me, Lord. You read my heart like an open book and You know all the words I'm about to speak before I even start a sentence! You know every step I will take before my journey even begins. Every single moment You are thinking of me! How precious and wonderful to consider that You cherish me constantly in Your every thought! O God, Your desires toward me are more than the grains of sand on every shore! When I awake each morning, You're still with me. Lord, You know everything there is to know about me. You perceive every movement of my heart and soul, and You understand my every thought before it even enters my mind.

You've gone into my future to prepare the way, and in kindness You follow behind me to spare me from the harm of my past. With your hand of love upon my life, You impart a blessing to me. This is just too wonderful, deep, and incomprehensible! Your understanding of me brings me wonder and strength. Where could I go from Your Spirit? Where could I run and hide from Your face? If I go up to heaven, You're there! If I go down to the realm of the dead, You're there too! If I fly with wings into the shining dawn, You're there! If I fly into the radiant sunset, You're there waiting! Wherever I go, Your hand will guide me; Your strength will empower me. It's impossible to disappear from You or to ask the darkness to hide me, for Your presence is everywhere, bringing light into my night. There is no such thing as darkness with You.

The night, to You, is as bright as the day; there's no difference between the two. You formed my innermost being, shaping my delicate inside and my intricate outside, and wove them all together in my mother's womb. I thank You, God, for making me so mysteriously complex! Everything You do is marvelously breathtaking. It simply amazes me to think about it! How thoroughly You know me, Lord! You even formed every bone in my body when You created me in the secret place, carefully, skillfully shaping me from nothing to something.

You saw who you created me to be before I became me! Before I'd ever seen the light of day, the number of days You planned for me was already recorded in Your book. God, I invite your searching gaze into my heart. Examine me through and through; find out everything that may be hidden within me. Put me to the test and sift through all my anxious cares. See if there is any path of pain I'm walking on, and lead me back to Your glorious, everlasting ways— the path that brings me back to You." Psalms 139:1-18, 23-24 TPT

A BONUS Prayer:

Holy Spirit, You have revealed things to me I did not know. Fears, feelings, worries, questions and emotions that have kept me from being completely free, You have shown to me. As You reveal to heal, please help me to turn to You, repent of faulty agreements I've made and help me keep priorities in order so I may experience Your true peace and love others as I love myself. As Your presence takes over God, I choose to take care of Your temple, my body that I carry you in. I repent that I have allowed it to become busy, exhausted and out of line when I take the things You lay on my heart and then I go beyond the realm of what You have given me to do. Help me Jesus, as I desire to be in step with You, moment by moment, walking by faith in Your love. You are faithful Lord, and I know that You began a good work in me and you are faithful and will carry it on to completion until the day You return. I trust You, Jesus! Suzanne

The journey is not always easy, but the destination makes it worth the trip.

CHAPTER 11

DEFINED AND IDENTIFIED

My prayer:

Father, may we be confident in who we are as sons and daughters of the Most High God. May we trust you as we sit in your lap and believe your promises over our life. I love you! Suzanne

There are things that have to be evaluated when we explore and seek inner healing. Under the direction of the Holy Spirit, Pastor Ron helped me gain revelation in our conversation that confirmed I had adapted false beliefs and had embraced fear deep within my soul. I acknowledged what the Lord revealed, and I repented of the fear and false beliefs as I stood in the gap and prayed an identification prayer of repentance on behalf of myself, and my family, those living and those to come. By embracing a new belief and thought through the power of the Holy Spirit, the sin of identifying with fear and the manifestations of it, are broken off of my life. I do not have to carry it any longer, and I refuse to remain in fear of fear.

I am disclosing some of the things I learned from Pastor Ron, some things I've acquired through research and some understanding I have gained through experience. Glean on this insight then research for yourself. Allow the Holy Spirit to guide you through your experiences to gain freedom and to change the future of generations to come because you dared to do so.

Where did that rotten root come from? Perhaps it didn't start with you.

Generational fear and sin

Fear or sin roots may have transferred to you through DNA, your environment or upbringing. If it exists or you believe you have been affected, it needs to be repented, even if the fear is rooted through generational fear or sin that has attached itself to you. It doesn't mean you have sinned, but the root originated in sin or someone else's fear, and has kept you attached to the fear it produced in you as a result, even if you were unaware of its existence. Remember, repentance simply means to turn away from an old way or thought and move towards a new one.

If others passed it down to you or placed it upon you, what can you do about it?

Identification Prayer of Repentance

When a person stands in the gap for their family, city, church or nation, and intercedes in prayer on their behalf, the prayer becomes one of identification. You become a representation through identification for the ones you are interceding for in their place. An ambassador or a representative receives or acts on behalf of the one/the unit/group/family/tribe/organization/business/government/city/state or nation they are representing. One person receives or acts on behalf of the whole.

This is the idea behind the identification prayer of repentance. You confess corporate sins to the Lord and ask Him to forgive the sins, and release the bonds that have kept those you are representing, under a curse because of the sin iniquity. Spiritually speaking, through prayer, you will denounce and break the curses and bondages you and those you are representing inherited and have become identified with. Ask the Lord to reveal these things to you and make sure you go through this process with the aid of a Christian mentor, minister or counselor. Do not do this alone. You may also request favor and blessings on behalf of those you identify with after repentance has been made. The blockage to the blessings has been removed so the favor may freely flow.

Though there is hope for healing, forgiveness and freedom in your inner being, Neil T. Anderson, author of the book, *The Bondage Breaker*, (page 240), explains clearly how and why you may be experiencing effects of fear or sin that you are indirectly identified with. "Iniquities can be passed on from one generation to the next if you don't renounce the sins of your ancestors and claim your new spiritual heritage in Christ. You are not guilty for the sin of any ancestor, but because of their sin, you may be vulnerable to satan's attack. Because of the fall, you are genetically predisposed to certain strengths or weaknesses and are influenced by the physical and spiritual atmosphere in which you were raised. These conditions can contribute toward causing someone to struggle with a particular sin.

Ask the Lord to show you specifically what sins are characteristic of your family by praying the following prayer: *"Dear Heavenly Father, I ask you to reveal to my mind now all the sins of my ancestors that are being passed down through family lines. I want to be free from those influences and walk in my new identity as a child of God.*

In Jesus name, amen."

Make sure you keep your prayer/faith journal handy and record what the Holy Spirit reveals to your mind when you ask Him to. Remember, He is for you and desires you to walk in wholeness and freedom with Him. When you ask the Lord to reveal things to you that He wants to cleanse and purify, He will do it but be patient, because the Lord knows the right timing, order, circumstance and situation that will be best for you. It may come in layers over time or you may receive a download of dirt He wants to deliver you from. His ways are higher than ours and you can trust Him. He knows what you can handle and how much. He also knows if you are ready to receive knowledge and if you are ready to forgive from your heart once you are made aware of things. He will guard your heart and mind in Christ Jesus, and He is a good Father, so He is looking out for you. Trust His process of purification and pruning in your life. Position yourself to receive your deliverance and inner healing. He will reveal what He desires to heal!

Remember, it is not in our own ability, wisdom, striving or effort that we are made whole. It is accomplished only through Jesus Christ who shed His blood to break the power of sin, and it is only through His cleansing blood that we can truly be free. He alone breaks the power of sin-cycles, false belief systems, and soul ties we've made with other people or "false-gods" we have created, consciously or unconsciously.

The Word of God is clear about these statements and beliefs regarding generational iniquities, bonds, false gods, and identification prayers of repentance on behalf of those we represent, oversee or are identified with. Here are a few examples and you can find many others with a little Bible research:

> ***Galatians 4:8, NLT*** *"Before you Gentiles knew God, you were slaves to so-called gods that do not even exist."*

> ***Ephesians 2:1-10 NIV*** *"As for you, you were dead in your transgressions and sins, in which you used to live when you followed the ways of this world and of the ruler of the kingdom of the air, the spirit who is now at work in those who are disobedient. All of us also lived among them at one time, gratifying the cravings of our flesh and*

following its desires and thoughts. Like the rest, we were by nature deserving of wrath. But because of his great love for us, God, who is rich in mercy, made us alive with Christ even when we were dead in transgressions—it is by grace you have been saved. And God raised us up with Christ and seated us with him in the heavenly realms in Christ Jesus, in order that in the coming ages he might show the incomparable riches of his grace, expressed in his kindness to us in Christ Jesus. For it is by grace you have been saved, through faith—and this is not from yourselves, it is the gift of God— not by works, so that no one can boast. For we are God's handiwork, created in Christ Jesus to do good works, which God prepared in advance for us to do."

Nehemiah 1:4-7 NIV *"When I heard these things, I sat down and wept. For some days I mourned and fasted and prayed before the God of heaven. Then I said: Lord, the God of heaven, the great and awesome God, who keeps his covenant of love with those who love him and keep his commandments, let your ear be attentive and your eyes open to hear the prayer your servant is praying before you day and night for your servants, the people of Israel. I confess the sins we Israelites, including myself, and my father's family, have committed against you. We have acted very wickedly toward you. We have not obeyed the commands, decrees and laws you gave your servant Moses."*

Jesus is our closest relative because we are brothers and sisters in Christ and co-heirs to His throne in the kingdom of God. See Hebrews 2:11, 17. He has legal rights to redeem us to the Father. We had been separated from Him because of sin. But through the shed blood on the cross, Jesus stood in the gap for us as our representative to buy our freedom from sin and restore our relationship with the Father. He exchanged His blood as an identification sacrifice for our penalty we owed for our personal sin and the sin nature we were born into, even though He Himself was without sin. He stood in the gap for us and took our place. Jesus is our kinsman-redeemer just as Boaz was to Ruth when he took her on as his bride and restored her dead husband's property and good name in exchange. We are the bride of Christ and will be eternally. We are therefore identified with Christ. He represented us on the cross so we share in His victory over sin. We have the authority of Christ dwelling in our spirits to represent our families and tribes in a prayer of repentance.

We do not have to nor should we embrace or agree with sinful behaviors or beliefs that were handed down to us through our identification in a family or group we belong to, but we often do. It is not inherently a bad thing to attach to a family identity statement, but it may be. This is where you need discernment or guidance from the Holy Spirit.

Some identifiers simply give you a sense of belonging but some statements can be foretelling of negative futures if you bond to a false belief. For instance, have you ever heard someone speak of their family or group with words like, "that's just the way we are," or "I was born into a family of_____" or "we are a family of doctors" or "we aren't that smart" or "we always get sick" or something else along those lines that bring awareness of an identification by means of blood, belonging or beliefs? These statements when embraced and believed, form ties that bind us together with them. Again, not all bonds are bad, but they are worth considering.

In the case of my husband's family, we often say, "The men in our family are all pilots." Getting a pilot's license was never a mandate or pushed, but we have observed that beginning with my father-in-law, Joe Grimaud, who started the trend as a USAF pilot and private aviator, so far, all the men of age in the line have at least taken a solo flight or completed their certification. They were indirectly through identification with the family, inspired by Joe to fly or at least give it a try. They have flown an airplane and have been identified with being in a family of pilots. It is not meant to put future pressure on any of the young men or alienate any of the ladies in the family from doing the same, but if not careful, a person may take on an identity they do not want, and attach a false belief that if they do not follow suit, they are not important or significant. That is simply not true, however, the devil could lie to them and say they do not measure up or are not a part of the clan, thereby alienating the one in order to set them up for a spiritual attack.

We also see beautiful manifestations of identification, like Joshua proclaimed, "As for me and my household, we will serve the Lord." Joshua 24:15 NIV Even though each member of his house had to make a personal decision, Joshua set the stage, the environment and the identification with others in his family that allowed them to enjoy the favor of the Lord as a benefit of serving the Lord no matter what.

My husband Greg and I went through Greg Gunn's Family-ID workshop training when our children were young. As a result, we developed a family identification statement we wanted our family for generations to be known for, to embrace and to live by. We had a beautiful scripted word adhesive made and we put the Grimaud Family-ID on the living room wall of our home as a statement for all to see and as a reminder of who we are as a family. Then we simply have intentionally aimed to live it out, though we don't quote the phrase out loud that often. It has been a subtle and probably more subliminal message we have taught more by our actions than by a declaration of words. Perhaps you've heard it said, "More is caught than taught." I would agree with that statement but I would add that you teach what you model when you practice what you preach. They go together and are best transferred when who you are flows freely from your heart.

It shouldn't surprise us but it has delighted us when we have heard how our adult children, Alana, Danica and Garrison have embraced and carried out the family mission on their own. Here is our family identification, or Family-ID, otherwise known as the Grimaud family mission statement: *"We give so that others may live!"*

We give our time, our talents, our possessions and our lives so that others may experience life. Sometimes we have given in the form of food or money to those we know or those we know of who are in need. We have all given up our beds, loaned cars, or given time to spend with someone who needed a friend in their time of need. We've had the opportunity to give towards missions and missionaries through donations we've contributed to and collected from others. And we have had the privilege of participating through traveling abroad and giving of our time and talents to share the gospel and meet physical needs.

Our family shares holidays and our family meals with non-family members and have taught the kids the value of giving freely with a generous heart. During the Christmas Season, they get more excited about who they are going to give to than they are excited about receiving what they are desiring for themselves. That blesses our hearts so much and we have been personally challenged by our kid's selfless attitudes.

I am not saying these things to draw attention to or point at us, but to point out that with intention, we said, "As for me and my household, we give so that others may live." It has been a choice we've taken to take the words of Jesus, and the model of His life to model ours after. The Word says the Lord loves a generous and cheerful heart. It doesn't matter how much we have to give, but what matters is are we willing to give of what we have and share it with others, as we trust Jesus to supply our needs.

He inspires in us what He requires of us and through an act of faith He causes things to line up in our favor so He can fill the requests that meet the needs of the receiver and the giver alike. He gets all the glory and we get to tell the story of His faithfulness and goodness. A cheerful giver makes the heart glad, and brings healing to the soul. Feeling depressed or alone? Give generously to others and be filled with happiness.

We do our best to not become so attached to things or plans that we are not free to give them up, and we have never had a regret when we have done so. The Lord blesses those who take care of others, and though it is not for the blessings we give, we have indeed received back so much more that we have given. He supplies our needs and as we freely give to others, as we have been freely given to, we all get to live in the benefits of the blessings of the Lord. We are simply conduits of His love & provision and as we share with others, we get the blessing of connecting them to the heart of the Father who provides all things. We get to tell them we gave to them because the Lord loves them so much and put them on our hearts. We get to show them what real abundant life looks like when they surrender their hearts to Christ.

We give of ourselves so we can give Christ to them. He lives in us and when we give to others, we are giving them Jesus. Now, this is an identity we have embraced and passed down that we hope and pray will travel to the generations that come behind us all the way to the return of Jesus. He is the source we are tied to and we are bonded to each other by His love. See the difference?

I hope this helps you get clarity on why it is important to explore attachments and identifications and determine if they are to be embraced or eradicated. Things that are innocent can be used against us to cause division and destruction to our homes because our enemy is out to kill, steal and destroy all things that are good.

But God! The Lord created all things good and for your good including your marriage, your children, your family, your identity, your future and your hope. So if you have put a false identity on someone else or if you have embraced one yourself, just repent of it and give yourself some grace. Change your words and embrace the truth so you can be the one to stand in the gap for your loved ones and break the sin-cycle while creating a new freedom-cycle for your tribe.

Remember, revelation carries responsibility with it and the Lord may have you in mind to be an ambassador of reconciliation for those you represent, including the generations to come. Are you willing to stand in the gap for others? You may be the key to unlocking freedom for generations that will follow behind you. I pray that all who come behind us find us faithful.

Seek the Father's heart and ask the Holy Spirit to give you revelation and confirmation if you are to intercede on behalf of your family or others with the knowledge He has unveiled to you. Then, before you do, consult a trusted Christian advisor to partner in prayer with you as you take the action steps of praying the identification prayer of repentance, and receive generational restoration and healing. That's a priceless inheritance worth passing down!

Trust His process of purification and pruning in your life. Position yourself to receive your deliverance and inner healing. He will reveal what He desires to heal!

CHAPTER 12

I GIVE YOU MY WORD

My prayer:

Lord, keep my ears open to hear Your Word, and help me guard the words of my mouth. May I remember to bring matters before You. You know all things and You keep Your promises, so let my words be few. Teach me Your ways and to acknowledge them in all that I do. I love You, Jesus! Suzanne

Years ago, business deals were made on a hand shake and this powerful phrase, "I give you my word!" because the words spoken were received as a binding promise. This is a strong statement that used to mean everything when spoken and received. The one who spoke the promise into existence was speaking out of integrity with intent of keeping the pledge made through the spoken word. This "word" held power and reflected intentions that were believed and binding. Today, however, it is rare to find legal agreements being made with "a man's word." They have been replaced with a thick stack of written documents with a lot of "mumble jumble" to guard the parties from being held liable for personal harm.

My husband and I are entrepreneurs with a national automotive franchise company, Precision Tune Auto Care. We have business partners, loans and agreements which require us to enter into these large legal agreements. Everytime I put my signature on the line, I secretly wonder if I am inadvertently signing away one of my children in case of default, because I assure you I have not read every word of that agreement personally. I would like to believe the bank would loan us the money to open a new business if Greg were to walk in, stick out his hand in an effort to shake on it, and say, "I promise to pay the loan back in full, on time, with interest. How about it? I give you my word." I can tell you, my transformed man of God is indeed a man of integrity and when he gives his word, he means it, but sadly, this bank scenario will never take place. It would bring a good laugh and make for a great memory though.

I am drawing attention to this because as a Christ follower, led by the Holy Spirit, and walking in the truth of God's Word, we are held to a higher standard than the world is. Jesus told His disciples to "let your yes be yes and your no be no." I realize in today's society, when we are speaking of legal matters, it is wise to get written documents and follow the path of wisdom. I am however talking about our motives and intentions when we make a promise. Our word, as a follower of Jesus, should mean everything. We are to live with integrity in our hearts, minds and in our words. We are to walk in purity and with power because we carry the presence of Christ in our earthly containers. Our words are powerful and they create blessings or cursings. Our words speak life or death. They edify others or bring destruction upon their heads. Another mystery of our word exists for ourselves. When we open our mouths and speak, our ears hear what has originated in our hearts. The words are then delivered to our soul which demands a response. We must choose to either agree with these created words and tuck them deep inside our core, or our soul rejects the words and spits them out.

Have you ever wondered why the Psalmist, King David, would say,

"Bless the Lord, O my soul…" or "Praise the Lord, O my soul…" I believe he was creating with his voice what he wanted his ears to deliver to his innermost being so that his soul would respond correctly. He was telling his own soul what to do. He was speaking positive words and was encouraging himself. Let's see how it sounds to flip the phrase around, "Soul of mine…Praise the Lord!" It sounds more like a command than an afterthought. And then as David's soul responded to his words and obeyed, out of his heart flowed the most beautiful response and in turn, his spirit was lifted up. *Psalms 103: 1-5 NLT* is a great example: *"Praise the Lord, my soul; all my inmost being, praise his holy name. Praise the Lord, my soul, and forget not all his benefits—who forgives all your sins and heals all your diseases, who redeems your life from the pit and crowns you with love and compassion, who satisfies your desires with good things so that your youth is renewed like the eagle's."*

"I give you my Word!" That's what He said …

… and that's exactly what God did for us. His Living Word, His son, Jesus, who has always been, and who created all things with His spoken Word, became flesh, and dwelt among us. God loved us so much that He gave up His only son, The Word, that by believing in Him, we would live eternally with Him. This living, breathing Word, is the incarnate Word of God, the Word John spoke of that was here in the beginning, and He is the Word that was foretold about in ancient Scriptures, and that was fulfilled and later written about in the gospels.

The sword of the Spirit, our armour weapon, is this Word of God. It is the fresh, life-giving, relevant, rhema, spoken Word of God and it is legal and binding. You can trust it. God is a man of His Word. He is the Word. He keeps His Word. He keeps His promises because He is the promise! And you can take this Word to the bank, guaranteed! The legal and binding promissory note of the Word of God will reap eternal dividends for your life. It delivers salvation, freedom, healing, hope and power to destroy the works of the enemy. According to *Hebrews 4:12 NLT*, this powerful Word of God weapon *"is alive and powerful. It is sharper than the sharpest two-edged sword, cutting between soul and spirit, between joint and marrow. It exposes our innermost thoughts and desires."*

A "Word" with three meanings …

There are three different definitions and usages for the word "Word" as found in the Bible. One of my favorite tools for researching the origins of biblical words is through the Blue Letter Bible app I frequently refer to on my phone. Understanding the original intent of words helps gain a deeper understanding and application of the scriptures. Sometimes verses just don't make sense, but through digging in a little deeper, I get a holy aha moment and suddenly, I'm amazed at the new level of wisdom I've received. The three different words for "word" are: rhema, grapho, and logos.

According to the Blue Letter Bible App, for *Ephesians 6:17, "the sword of the Spirit, which is the Word of God,"* is referring to the rhema word of God.

"Word" Meaning #1:

A rhema (Word) is that which is or has been uttered by a living voice, thing spoken, word or saying as in a message. A rhema word is common in the New Testament when the Lord speaks His dynamic living word into a believer; to prophesy living words from the Lord to another person; or a word or saying spoken directly to you from the Lord. When a Christ follower is filled with the indwelling presence of the Holy Spirit, the Spirit also often speaks a rhema word to the heart, sometimes in a "knowing," an inward "hearing" or thought. Another way a rhema word is delivered to the believer's heart is when studying the written Word of God, the Spirit highlights a verse or passage and quickens your heart with understanding, conviction, comfort, revelation or wisdom. He takes the written Word and gives you a rhema Word for your current situation, and you increase in faith, courage and belief. The word may be for you but it is probably for you as well as others in the body of Christ to be encouraged by. Share it and see if you are right. Many times you'll find you are confirming and edifying what the Spirit is speaking to the hearts and minds of others. After all, we prophesy in part, and we need each other to know how to move forward in unity. If you receive a rhema Word of God that He wants you to release to another person or group of Christ followers, the Word is an active living Word for all who will hear and receive it unto themselves as well. Romans 10:17 NKJV tells us, "So then, faith comes from hearing, and hearing by the (Rhema) word of God."

Since the sword of the Spirit is the rhema Word of God, then a fresh spoken living Word of God is your mighty weapon, sharper than a two edged sword, penetrating even to dividing soul and spirit, joints and marrow. The rhema Word of God judges the thoughts and attitudes of the heart. The rhema Word is alive, active and powerful. It is our weapon but only if we use it. Jesus makes a spoken word and His written Word come alive to you when He breathes life to the Word. There is life and power in the Word to accomplish what the Lord wills to do through it.

On May 21, 1988, Greg and I gave our covenant rhema word to each other in marriage, promising to be faithful, to love, to cherish, in sickness and in health, in good times and in bad...as long as we both shall live. Of course, you're at a point in this story that you can see that not all of this sacred vow has been kept, but because of the grace of God, and the forgiveness made for us and through us by way of Jesus, our vows & commitment have been renewed and restored. Hallelujah!

After we had come through about five years of our "new" vow keeping way of life, we chose to privately exchange our vows to one another again. We have friends who have done this publicly as like a second wedding, but we chose to do it with the witness of a few friends, instead. We took the savings, and invested in a new wedding ring for me and we took a trip to Destin to a couples only beach Bed and Breakfast, which has become a special annual tradition for us, though 2020 has changed this year's plans. I had bought Greg a new wedding ring for his birthday in January, 2005, because it was significant for me to speak to his heart that I was willing to walk a new path with him.

Vows are important and when we mess up and break them, we have the choice to acknowledge our mistakes, repent, confess, and renew our commitments to one another. I can say with so much confidence that our word is holding true because the true Word is holding us true to our word. The truth has set us free. He is faithful and true, and we have been too. Praise the Lord...O my soul!

The spoken rhema, living Word of God...still speaks to and through the people of God who are living under the influence of the Holy Spirit! And when we agree with and speak the written Word of God, power is released to and through the sons and daughters of the Most High God.

"Word" Meaning #2:

A grapho (Word) is the written word. In Matthew 4:4, when Jesus said, "It is written..." three times to the devil to withstand his temptations, he was referring to the grapho Word of God found in the Scriptures. He referred to the grapho word, but it was a rhema word the Holy Spirit quickened to Jesus at the time of need when He took authority and commanded satan to "Get out of here!" When Jesus spoke a rhema command, the devil was forced to flee. Because Jesus modeled for us what to do when we are tempted, and because His Spirit abides in us, when we are tempted, we too can apply the grapho word, and allow the Holy Spirit to speak a rhema word, as we take the authority Christ gave us. The enemy will have to flee our presence as well. When we who believe in the Word of God (God's son, Jesus, who has always been), saturate in the written Word of God (the Grapho, Holy Bible) and are transformed by renewing our mind in it, then we, the redeemed, receive and release the spoken living Word of God (by the power of the Holy Spirit), which allows God to do greater works through our willing obedience, to accomplish His will on the earth. This is all to bring His Kingdom down to earth as it is in Heaven, to restore all things to Himself — for our good and for His glory, for all eternity — for the sake of oneness and fellowship between man and God the Father, God the Son and God the Holy Spirit.

"Word" Meaning #3:

A logos (Word) is a Word, not in a mere grammatical sense, but when uttered by a living voice, embodies an idea or a conceived thought. It derives from the Greek word, lego. It is also referred to as a divine expression. In John 1:1, "In the beginning was the Word...." the word, Word is logos. The logos was in the beginning, "and the Word (logos) was with God, and the Word (logos) was God. We know God is Father, Son, and Holy Spirit, the three in one, often referred to as the Trinity (logos). The logos Word of God has always existed. We may not fully understand it or Him as no mind can conceive, but by faith, we believe it to be true and we believe and trust in the one true God. Jesus came to the earth as an expression of the Father. The (logos) Word became flesh and dwelt among us.

The "Kingdom of God" is also logos, as found in *Matthew 13:19 NLT*. "When anyone hears the word (logos) of the kingdom, and does not understand it, then the wicked one comes and snatches away what was sown in his heart." What was sown? It was the seed of the Word (logos) that was snatched. We have to activate our faith to believe in the logos and in so doing, the seed is planted in fertile ground and we keep the seed buried deep within our being. The Lord waters it and causes it to grow in our hearts, which nourishes our minds.

Even though the sword of the Spirit Word of God is a rhema Word, the concept of the armour of God is rather a logos Word. By the Word, we believe the Word, and He speaks a Word as we act on the Word. Our weapon is the Word of God, and it is mighty to break strongholds, demolish arguments that present itself against the knowledge of God, and the weapon brings healing to our bones and to our brains. Regardless of how hurt you may have been in this evil world, the body, soul and mind are healed when you take up and activate the sword of the Spirit, which is the Word of God!

As I complete this section on a beautiful Sunday morning, I find it appropriate to read and agree on this song of David, found in *Psalms 92*. We started out this chapter with instructions from Paul to speak words of truth and encouragement to one another. We are to sing songs, psalms and inspired songs of praise to our awesome God. We are to talk about the Lord when we rise till when we sleep. Then all through the night, our soul will continue to praise the Lord. When we speak the Word of truth with our mouths and when we believe it and agree in our hearts, and then when we join our songs with other believers in Jesus Christ, our praise becomes a powerful weapon in the heavenly realms.

With our swords raised high, we are able together, as the unified body of Christ, to stand firm, to tear down strongholds, and to destroy the chaos accompanied by our enemy, by way of the Shalom Peace of God. So join in the powerful praise chorus as you read this written Word of God. He gave us His Word as an everlasting gift so let's unite in spirit, truth and love and let's give the Lord our gift of thanksgiving. Let's put Holy Spirit power to this Word and usher in the Kingdom of God as one voice. After all, we the soldiers of Christ, hurt in this sinful world, are in this unified body of Christ together; and as we work in unity, bonded by love, we receive our full healing, by the healing Word of God!

By His word, I give my word ...

When we pray through the Word, we bring our petitions to the feet of Jesus. But after we have brought them to Him, it is time to thank Him in advance for what He is going to do and for all He has already done. I've heard it said that praying through, then praising through is the key that opens the door to your breakthrough. So, what are you waiting for? Let's give God our word by the power of His healing, living Word, uniting together as one voice, and let's get our praise on!

A Sunday Morning Song of Praise
By King David, Psalms 92

"It's so enjoyable to come before You with uncontainable praises spilling from our hearts! How we love to sing our praises over and over to You, to the matchless God, high and exalted over all! At each and every sunrise we will be thanking You for Your kindness and Your love. As the sun sets and all through the night, we will keep proclaiming, "You are so faithful!" Melodies of praise will fill the air as every musical instrument, joined with every heart, overflows with worship. No wonder I'm so glad; I can't keep it in! Lord, I'm shouting with glee over all You've done, for all You've done for me!

What mighty miracles and Your power at work, just to name a few. Depths of purpose and layers of meaning saturate everything You do. Such amazing mysteries found within every miracle that nearly everyone seems to miss. Those with no discernment can never really discover the deep and glorious secrets hidden in Your ways. It's true the wicked flourish, but only for a moment, foolishly forgetting their destiny with death, that they will all one day be destroyed forevermore.

But You, O Lord, are exalted forever in the highest place of endless glory, while all Your opponents, the workers of wickedness, will all perish, forever separated from You. Your anointing has made me strong and mighty. You've empowered my life for triumph by pouring fresh oil over me. You've said that those lying in wait to pounce on me would be defeated, and now it's happened right in front of my eyes and I've heard their cries of surrender!

Yes! Look how You've made all your lovers to flourish like palm trees, each one growing in victory, standing with strength! You've transplanted them into Your heavenly courtyard, where they are thriving before You. For in Your presence they will still overflow and be anointed. Even in their old age they will stay fresh, bearing luscious fruit and abiding faithfully. Listen to them! With pleasure they still proclaim: "You're so good! You're my beautiful strength! You've never made a mistake with me."" Psalms 92:1-15TPT

The legal and binding promissory note of the Word of God will reap eternal dividends for your life. It delivers salvation, freedom, healing, hope and power to destroy the works of the enemy.

CHAPTER 13

PEACE & QUIET

My prayer:

Lord, I always need your peace and you know I need your quiet rest for my soul. Help me receive the peace that only comes from you. Lord, I also ask that you would take my testimony of how you have provided this peace and quiet to bring a fresh new stability to my mind, and use it to give hope to your children who are praying for peace. I pray your Spirit would be infused with theirs and they would find rest for their souls. You said as recorded in Matthew 11:28–30 NIV, "Come to me, all you who are weary and burdened, and I will give you rest. Take my yoke upon you and learn from me, for I am gentle and humble in heart, and you will find rest for your souls." So with that, I come. I love you! Suzanne

If you haven't noticed by now, I am starting the chapters in this section with a prayer, much like my prayers I record in my secret place. My faith prayer journals are filled with dialogues with the Father, scriptures He highlights to me, and notes of revelation, insight, wisdom and questions. The Word says to pray without ceasing, and it's my interpretation that we are to have an ongoing conversation with the Lord all day long. In my journals, I randomly switch from writing my cares to casting them on Him as I speak to Jesus in prayer. A prayer journal is a great way to intentionally take time to sit quietly at the feet of Jesus and let Him pour out His peace upon your head and into your heart. It is a calming tool He taught me before I knew I would even need it. He is our provider and He meets all our needs, including a space for personal intimate relationship with Himself.

The Apostle Peter reminds us in *I Peter 5:7 NIV to, "cast all your cares on Him, for He cares for you."* God not only cares for you, but He carries our heavy loads of concern. As a wife and a mother of three wonderful grown kids, I still find that I am tempted to pick up the load of care from them and try to carry it again. But when I choose to cast it on the Father, He replaces my cares with His rest. I know that as much as I love and want to protect my children, God loves them more and is a better caregiver of all His children than we could ever be. I trust Him. Sometimes I need to remind my soul what to do. "Trust God," I tell myself.

When I am tempted to worry, I bundle up my worries and let Jesus carry the package, and then I choose to pray instead. I activate my faith by the power of the Holy Spirit in me that enables me to choose joy instead of worry. *"It is God working in me to will and to do for his good pleasure," as Paul tells me in Philippians 2:3.* When I dwell in the Lord, He works through me and together, we co-labor as He works to will and accomplish all He desires for His glory. I get to share in His glory as He establishes His Kingdom, delivers me from evil and delivers good to His children. I think we sure make it harder than it has to be because we often think it is by our own effort and ability that we achieve success and receive favor from the Lord. But it is in fact none of that.

As Paul reflects in *Philippians 3: 7-11*, he considers all things worthless and as garbage in comparison to knowing Christ Jesus as Lord and in becoming one with Him. I too count on Christ to save me and I believe by faith that God has made me right with Him because of Jesus. There is no comparison to knowing Jesus and becoming one with Him. Because of this reality, I know Christ and experience His power working in my life. I rejoice knowing I am full of the joy of the Lord. This joy is accompanied by peace and gentleness: a gift of quietness to my soul.

A Natural remedy prescription ...

What is the long term remedy for victory over worry, fear, panic, anxiety and depression? In my humble opinion based on experience and in standing on the truth of God's Word, I believe the cure is to be found in the "peaceful, quiet rest of God." Once you enter His rest and choose to abide in it, He will provide the rest of what you need to be delivered from the cares you once carried. His presence carries the fullness of God in it and it activates all Jesus paid for to provide freedom, healing and hope for your restless heart. I am also an advocate for seeking professional help and medical assistance if necessary, but the root cause demands for a root cure and the only remedy that can get to the root properly is the deep penetrating hand of God that can rip it out and pour healing into the wound. He is the natural source for everlasting healing.

If you will remain in the peaceful quiet rest of God, He will work the rest out for your good and for His good and glorious pleasure. It is His will to accomplish and do this in you. It pleases Him to do so but as the Lord is a gentleman, He waits for us to wait upon Him and to want Him to complete His work in our lives.

Paul said it well regarding what we do with our past once we encounter Jesus. He said to forget about the past and press on towards what lies ahead in our future. You can read all about it in *Philippians 3:12-14*, but how do you do what he said?

Paul's advice regarding our past, present and future:

Past -   Forget it - Leave it in the past.

Present - Press on - Move forward in faith.

Future - Expect it to be glorious because faith in God assures it. He works all things for our good and His glory and that is a promise from God. He gives us hope for a future with Him.

Practically speaking, here are some ways you can put Paul's words into practice regarding dealing with fear, grief, anxiety and trauma. I took his advice and wrote out my own words as I've applied the Word to my life and the situations I've faced.

Past -   In the past, I used to embrace and dwell in fear which developed into worry, anxiety, panic, depression and the need to control.

Present - But now, I daily cast my cares on Jesus and walk by faith, fully armored in my Spiritual battle gear. I'm prepared to participate with God by His Spirit's leading and working in my life moment by moment. I choose every day to praise the Lord and trust Him.

Future -   I will walk faith-filled, joy-filled, healed and restored. I am in a growing relationship with God, through His son, Jesus. I am equipped by love and I walk in forgiveness. I am free to forgive, live and love as a child of God. I walk in freedom and I have hope for my future. I anticipate tomorrow because I trust in Jesus.

How to leave yesterday in the past and hope for tomorrow: "But one thing I do: Forgetting what is behind and straining toward what is ahead, I press on toward the goal to win the prize for which God has called me heavenward in Christ Jesus." Philippians 3:13b-14 NIV

In the space below, or in your prayer journal, try this exercise for yourself. What has been in your <u>past</u> that you need to leave behind? Acknowledge it and write it down. Try to be specific. Remind yourself what you are doing in the <u>present</u> to act on your faith. And then declare or prophesy to your <u>future</u> what you will experience as a result of pressing forward towards it. Before you begin to write, pause and ask the Holy Spirit to give you wisdom, insight and His plan for you to carry this out. Then listen. Write what comes to your mind.

Past -

_____

_____

_____

_____

Present -

_____

_____

_____

_____

Future -

_____

_____

_____

_____

A God Plan of Action For Immediate Action! ...

After you record your thoughts regarding your past, present and future, I have some other suggestions from scripture to help you to be successful in carrying out your strategic plan of action of pressing forward and looking with hope to your future. Try these things and add what you find works for you. I will also share some practical tips that have helped me to achieve a calm state of mind when I've needed some help.

We are all fashioned in His image, but we have different personalities and ways in which we respond and operate best because we truly are uniquely and wonderfully made. However, there are some things the Lord gave us in the Word that applies to everyone so we must try our best to do as He said so we can receive all He has in store for our lives. Before we explore anything else, let's look at what the Bible tells us will provide stability to our minds in need of peace, quiet and rest.

Six scripture based action steps to achieve stability, security & peace of mind:

1. Put your armour on every single day before you take a step.

Think through each piece of the God suit and speak it out loud. Remind your soul that you are getting dressed and suited for battle. To stand, put the full armour on. A stable foundation requires a standing position so get suited up for stability and stand!

2. Start and end each day with a thankful heart and a voice of praise!

Speak to Jesus in the morning and tell Him thank you for the gift of salvation. By faith, tell the Lord thank you for your healing (even if it hasn't fully manifested yet). Tell God how much you love Him and how wonderful He is to you. Let Him know you recognize His goodness, His mercies, His compassions, His faithfulness and His holiness! Tell your soul to praise the Lord, just like King David did. Then do it! Say it! "Praise you, Jesus!" Before you go to sleep, thank Him for the blessings of the day. Let Christ know you are wanting to grow in your relationship with Him. Tell Him what is on your heart and be grateful for all He has done. A grateful and thankful heart is a happy heart! Try it!

If you love music, and even if you don't, fill your home, your car, your mind and your day with a song of praise. In Old Testament battles, the tribe of Judah lead the way before the weaponed warriors because they were the praisers, and praise leads the way to victory! As a result, confusion would enter the enemy's camp and the enemy would fight themselves. When the Israelites arrived on the scene, the battle was over and they were instructed to go get the goods. The Lord fights our battles when we pray and when we praise. God inhabits the praise of His people and in the Lord's army, praise is the mighty weapon that destroys strongholds and brings the breakthrough. So get your praise on and sing your heart out to God. Shift the spiritual atmosphere around you by filling the airwaves with worship and praise, and watch things change.

3. Activate your faith and take steps as though you see what you believe.

Do not be tempted to believe a negative report. You may have to opt not to turn on the news, or choose not to scroll through your favorite social feeds, except for a limited time you allow for. Activate your faith by choosing to believe what you know to be true regardless of what you hear, feel and see. Remember, the unseen realm is your true reality. What is seen with your eyes that is troubling you is caused by the sinful effects of the prince of this world. So, do not be anxious, worried, troubled or afraid because of what you see and understand with your natural mind. Again, the Bible's definition of faith is found in *Hebrews 11:1 NIV, "Now faith is being sure of what we hope for and certain of what we do not see."* Our faith is activated when we confidently take steps of action as though we believe what we are hoping for by faith. Ask the Holy Spirit to take the steps with you and you will not be walking alone. We walk by faith, not by sight.

4.   Renew your mind with heavenly thoughts every day.

We receive a transformed life by the renewing of our minds. We are to think on things that God thinks about and on the things He has spoken about us. God is love and He loves you. Think about that. It is a statement of truth and one worth pondering over. Paul tells us what to think about in *Phillipians 4:8 NIV, "Finally, brothers and sisters, whatever is true, whatever is noble, whatever is right, whatever is pure, whatever is lovely, whatever is admirable--if anything is excellent or praiseworthy--think about such things."*

We know the Word of God was inspired by God and is a living Word of God, so if we read in the Word of God instructions on what to do and what to think about, we can rest assured that it is worth acting upon. The Word of God is in and of itself a heavenly thought. God is in heaven and if He thinks it, it is a heavenly thought. Think about that. You can think about heaven as a place you will spend eternity in, and that is something definitely worth thinking about. It will be amazing, I promise, and I am excited that I will be spending eternity there. Thinking heavenly thoughts though is easier than you might have thought when you include thinking about what is true, pure, lovely, admirable and praiseworthy in the mix. There are so many good things we can fill our minds with but we have to eliminate the thoughts that are opposite of these thoughts to have space in our minds for them.

Be reminded Dr. Caroline Leaf says that when we eliminate toxic thoughts and replace them with positive true thoughts based on the Bible, and we speak them every day, we begin to believe the new thoughts. After 21 days of this toxic thought detox, the neuron connections literally eradicate the toxic thought that was causing harm to the body, and it is replaced by the healthy one which commands a positive response in the brain.

The mind has told the spirit what to align with and the brain receives the signals to heal itself as a byproduct. So when we read in the Bible we are to be transformed by the renewing of our minds, it is truly possible to achieve this miracle manifested in our bodies because we believe the Word of God to be true. It proves itself as truth.

5. Breathe in the peace of Jesus - and do not be afraid.

We are told in the Word to remain calm for the Lord fights for us. Well, one way you can help bring calmness to your anxious mind is to breathe deeply. May I suggest you sit still and intentionally slow down your breathing rhythm then call out to Jesus and receive deep breaths of His peace. Over and over again, we read that Jesus said, " Do not fear!" The angels always began their instructions with the words, "Do not be afraid!" The Word of God is laced with this command all throughout, "Do not fear!" The Holy Spirit whispers to our hearts, "Do not be afraid, for I am with you."

The crazy thing is even worldly culture tells us to not fear. There is a healthy fear we should all have that gives a level of protection in times of danger but I am talking about the everyday coping in life that is crippling when we are accompanied by fear. The world wants peace of mind but it does not know how to find this peace that combats fear. But we know where to find it. It is a gift from Jesus that is given to all who receive Him as Savior. He said, *"Peace I leave with you; My peace I give you. I do not give as the world gives. Do not let your hearts be troubled and do not be afraid."* This truth is found in *John 14:27 NIV*. Make sure to say thank you to Jesus for this wonderful peace of mind that He gives you even when everything around you seems to be falling apart or feels unstable. His peace is our stability that we put on our feet when we put our armour on. Wearing stable shoes of peace, we calmly stand, void of fear.

The peace of Jesus is far more wonderful than the human mind can understand or try to explain. His peace will guard your hearts and minds as you live in Christ Jesus. Take Paul's word for it found in the fourth chapter of Philippians and take my word for it, too. I can't explain or comprehend the His peace, but I also don't deny this truth for it has held me secure and has helped me to remain calm when waves of confusion have formed around me.

The peace of God has been my sustaining rock during all my times of mental trouble. At times, when I have physically been shaking in my body, and things around me have shaken from underneath me, my mind has remained at perfect peace. When storms of worry have surfaced in my spirit, the peace of God has surrounded me and has soothed my anxious thoughts. When chaos has been created and has manifested through fear, frustrations, malicious talk or confusion around me, I have literally done what Jesus did and have spoken to the storms, out loud, *"Peace! Be Still!"* As a result, I have heard people to immediately resolve their arguments and I have powerfully destroyed the fear within my mind of imminent danger because I took authority over it as Jesus commanded His disciples to do. I have also heard wild winds stop at the release of peace and the command to be still. I have slept through thunderstorms that rocked the house because I was anchored in the rock that poured out His peace when I asked for it.

The Shalom Peace of God carries authority in it to destroy chaos. If you are wearing the gospel shoes of peace, you too can walk in this same authority. This is how we walk by faith, because we are wearing beautiful powerful shoes which were given to us as a gift from Jesus. No wonder I love shoes so much--they symbolize God's peace!

6. Read the Word of God every day (I prefer mornings).

We are powered up by the Word of God. It is our foundation, our measuring rod/plumb line and is one of the main ways the Holy Spirit speaks to our hearts for edification, encouragement and instruction. When I start the day by seeking the Lord through His Word, I find that I get more done, and I am more productive. I also find I am at rest in my spirit and things don't irritate me as much as they would have if I had not filled up my spiritual tank before going about my day. Find what works best for your schedule and don't shy away from being creative. There are Bible Apps that read to you if you prefer to listen while you get dressed or drive to work. Perhaps that's how you can start your morning, then later in the day or evening, you might find a time to open up your physical Bible and saturate yourself in it. Consider these words of Jesus found in *Matthew 6:33 ESV, "But seek first the Kingdom of God and His righteousness, and all these things will be added unto you."* There is an order to things because we serve an orderly God, and He wants to be at the top of our list.

I've heard experts in the field of psychology say that to achieve stability you must first work to acknowledge and embrace your fears to properly deal with them before you can bring them into a space for spiritual healing. Though I am not an expert, I disagree with this belief because of personal experience and from reading the Word of God. Though these things may hold an amount of truth, I do believe the order is presented backwards. My belief is there are layers and steps of bringing the mind to health and I also believe in the practice of practical steps that most experts seem to agree on. I have put many of the steps to the test and they have been helpful. However, when we attempt to do things by leaning on our own strength, abilities, understanding and wisdom, we see we have fallen short of the glory of God.

We tend to feel a gravitational pull towards that which we focus our attention on. Have you ever noticed your car getting out of the lane when you look at something to your side? If you dread something, the thoughts of dread will consume you and cause you to remain in fear of it. Our fears work like a magnet, pulling us close until we feel bonded to them. Embracing that which we need to be freed from, as the experts say, only serves to ensure the bond grip to the thing we are embracing and as a result, the bond grows tighter. The only thing that can break that tight grip is the powerful bond breaking, cleansing blood of Jesus applied to it.

If we bring our bonds of anxiety to Christ, the power of the cross of Jesus will break the bond we have made with fear, and it will be loosened from our soul. Once free, we are free to focus on staying free, receiving deeper inner healing and deliverance through the help of a Holy Spirit led counselor or ministry, and we can apply practical steps to renew our minds and enjoy mental health as a way of life.

If we intentionally live in the peace of God and enjoy quiet rest in His presence, the other pieces required to bring us into wholeness and healing will fall into place as we seek instruction from the Lord. He is a good Father and He desires good for his children. He will not withhold His love or tender mercies from you. He will satisfy all your needs including mental health and He will be your portion when you are filled with Him. He is your peace and He provides peace of mind for His people. His peace that surpasses all understanding will surely guard your heart and your mind, in Christ Jesus! Lock eyes with Jesus and receive the transfer of His peace deposited into your soul because His peace is the missing piece we need to enjoy real lasting peace of mind and quiet rest. My mind is set on His face, is yours?

If you will remain in the peaceful quiet rest of God, He will work the rest out for your good and for His good and glorious pleasure.

CHAPTER 14

ABOLISH ANXIETY AND RELAX

My Prayer:

Lord, I praise you because you are worthy of all praise. I'm locking my eyes on your eyes so I will not be distracted by all the chaos going on around me. My mind is fixed on you, Jesus, and I know you will keep my mind in perfect peace. Thank you for abolishing anxiety from my life by delivering me from the evil spirit of fear. You are faithful to your Word so have your way in me, Lord. I love this Word found in Philippians 4: 4-7 NLT: "Rejoice in the Lord always. I will say it again: Rejoice! Let your gentleness be evident to all. The Lord is near. Do not be anxious about anything, but in every situation, by prayer and petition, with thanksgiving, present your requests to God. And the peace of God, which transcends all understanding, will guard your hearts and your minds in Christ Jesus." I love you! Suzanne

There was a day I embraced a false belief that anxiety is something only a few people carry around. Before you experience something for yourself, you are unaware, and it is easy to think what you are going through is somehow an isolated case. It is not until you openly confess what is happening in your own mind, that you realize you truly are not alone. It is a sad discovery though because anxiety, grief and depression is a hard place to reside, regardless of how long you are there, and even though you find you're not alone, you also grieve that someone else has suffered the way you have. At least this realization has the power to produce compassion in your heart for others in perhaps a way you did not have before.

Anxiety is not something I continuously live with but as a result of allowing thoughts and fears to manipulate my mind from time-to-time in the past, and because I in turn focused on those thoughts or fears, I've inadvertently allowed panic attacks, irrational fears, and depression to appear in my life, as anxiety tried to "take me out." In another chapter, I share in detail how I was healed at the core and now live in freedom from fear which is, by the way, the root of anxiety. I had to get to the root of the issues that produced the fear in the first place and allow the Lord to deliver me from thoughts, beliefs, mindsets, strongholds, and struggles I was unaware I owned.

Please know that you are not stuck in the cycle you may find yourself in. There is hope in Jesus to break you free from these destructive mindsets, but there are also practical steps to help walk you out of the place you have felt stuck in. The stories in the Bible all show how Jesus healed, but He also required participation from the one receiving it, remember? Get up! Go! Walk! So we shall believe in Him and we shall also get up and walk out of this sticky place, by faith. For the spiritual side of hope over anxiety, which is the real hope, please spend time in some of the other chapters. In this chapter, I want to highlight practical steps I have learned to use that you can do to calm yourself, practice mindfulness, make your body obey and respond to your commands and finally abort anxiety.

The fear of fear ...

I used to fear a return of fear, which kept me bound to it, but I no longer feel afraid because I have taken an abolitionist approach to fear by identifying it, dealing with the root and letting the Lord abolish it from my life. Fear. You can't ignore it; you can't go around it; you can't go under and you must not bury it. But when you go through it, if you'll put your faith over it, and place it under the feet of Jesus, He will free you from the bondage of it. Hallelujah!

We are going to address what anxiety is, what causes it to take root, surface and pop up unexpectedly, and we will also address some tools to help you manage the manifestations of it while you are learning to live free of it. It may take some time to work through this and it may not take much time, but one thing I know is that it is time to take back your life and live free of anxiety because it does not belong to you. It is just hanging around and it has to go! Remember, the root of anxiety is fear which originates from your spiritual enemy, and fear is a liar. Fear is overcome by faith so when faith arises, fear has to flee. If the root of fear is pulled up and replaced by faith, then what grows will no longer be anxiety, but will instead be a root of peace.

The world verses the Word ...

The world calls anxiety a disorder (a disease) that you "have" but it is actually a distraction that you have been deceived by. The Word gives the remedy as Paul says, *"Do not be anxious about anything, but in every situation, by prayer and petition, with thanksgiving, present your requests to God." Philippians 4:6 NIV* If you are distracted by anxiety (which deceives you into thinking it is yours), turn your thoughts away from it because we are to be anxious for nothing, and focus on the face of Jesus (which centers you). Put your mind on Jesus as you pray and petition to Him, thanking Him and requesting He keep your mind at perfect peace as He fills your heart and mind with His thoughts. Think upon the fact that you are a son or daughter of God, loved dearly, held in the arms of Jesus and you are on His mind. He loves you and He understands what you are going through. Just imagine curling up into his lap, laying your head against His chest, and not having any cares because you are protected. Your "heavenly dad" is bigger than anything coming against you and you can take confidence that you can rest in His presence in a place of safety, security and of stability. Seriously, ignore your enemy, walk away from him and fix your gaze on Jesus. Receive His peace, remain calm and get some rest.

A portrait of anxiety ...

To better understand anxiety, we need to define it. Clinically speaking, according to the National Institute of Mental Health, a generalized anxiety disorder (GAD), is characterized by a "steady state of fear or worry" usually surrounding work, family, or health. This type of anxiety occurs usually for 6 months or more and carries symptoms of restlessness, fatigue, irritability, etc. It is typically difficult to control as its source is often undefined. Other forms of anxiety may be easier for doctors to diagnose and treat. The type of anxiety I've experienced is not of an ongoing GAD but has instead caught us all by surprise as fear has found a way in and formed panic attacks and irrational phobias.

Panic Attacks...

Panic attacks are unexpected periods of intense fear that come on suddenly and are accompanied by symptoms such as sweating, trembling, a racing heart or feelings of "impending doom." They can cause people to feel as if they are going insane or are somehow detached from themselves, according to the Diagnostic and Statistical Manual of Mental Disorders (DSM), which is the handbook that doctors rely on to identify and diagnose mental health conditions. There is much room for interpretation and understanding as some occurrences take place due to an isolated situation, a toxic environment or an overwhelming experience rather than by an inherited long-term problem.

For me, I have either been suddenly gripped by irrational fear, or I have felt and heard a snap occur in my brain as a disconnect, or I have suddenly awoken from my sleep with an urgent intense fear and verbal response to it. In all of these cases, I was caught off guard and thrown into panic. One time, my body went the route of "flight" and I found myself heading out the front door and escaping to the neighbor's porch before turning around and coming home. I have also taken the route of "<u>fight</u>" as I instinctively have gone into spiritual battle, though I have not physically fought anyone. And I have also had my body just "<u>freeze</u>" as I did not know what was happening.

Each of these responses are frightening if you are going through them, but if you can force yourself to recognize what is happening, you can also accept the reality that it is not going to last and that your loved ones who are also experiencing it with you, are trying to help you rather than hurt you. Things will go better for you if you will allow them to help you. Your honesty with them and your effort to allow their help, will help them trust you so they may help you to get the help you need. If you resist to cooperate, it may not go well for you, in your current state of mind. I have always found it is better to trust the Lord to help my husband and loved ones help me. With a temporary onset of "lack of trust in others," it's best to trust God to guide them to help me remain calm. This has been possible because it is the way I live when in total health. Who you are and what is inside of you before the battles is who you are and what will come out of you when in the fight.

Phobias...

This is a specific identified intense fear or worry tied to an animal, activity, situation, or another source that is easy to define. The most common phobia shared with the majority of healthy people is that of speaking in public, for instance. Some people have a phobia of heights, being in tight places, or have a fear of flying. If you suffer from being anxious about these things but do them anyways, it is not considered a disorder; however, if you rearrange your life to avoid them, it may be an indicator of a bigger problem. The dysfunction of anxiety may trigger negative symptoms that disrupt your life, and will reveal your need to seek professional help.

For me, there have been specific new fears that have hit

me out of nowhere when I have been thrown into a period of anxiety. These episodes have lasted anywhere from three days to a few weeks. I am not a fan of listing fears the enemy has gripped me with because I no longer am afraid and I do not wish to give any glory to the devil. But I will say that by faith, I have faced each fear every time as I begin to regain balance in my brain. When I am able, I pick up my mat, I walk, I go and put my faith to the test. As I do, God meets me there and trashes the fear that was testing my faith. I am an overcomer through the blood of the Lamb, the word of my testimony and because even though some of my fears were huge, I was not afraid even unto death. I've put my trust in God and He has triumphed over all fear that has come against me, and I have been left standing in the peace of God.

Are you stressed or are you anxious? What's the difference? Stress is the source of anxiety. For example: You may be in a hurry because you are late, behind in a project or had an interruption that set you back and off schedule. You may have been able to avoid the situation, or you may have had something happen to you beyond your control that has put you in this scenario. Regardless of how you got there, stress has now given you a reason to experience anxiety. When you are anxious, you may feel worry because you think of all the negative possibilities that could happen because of your situation, and your impending fearful outcome fuels the anxiety stirring inside you. Your body then takes over because it is going to protect you. Your emotional alarm system goes off and your internal first responder kicks into action, sometimes kicking you in the behind causing panic to set in. Out of nowhere, there you are, so it seems, under attack.

For me, I have personally experienced a variety of symptoms in my body when I have had an episode of panic erupt. It is hard to pinpoint these things ahead of time because some of the symptoms happen due to other circumstances. Usually, when anxiety is present and active, there will be multiple symptoms that hit the body all at once. The problem is you most likely will not realize it until after anxiety has unleashed the fury in the form of an unexpected panic attack.

Some physical manifestations of anxiety that might emerge as a response to fear:

- A flood of hormones being released into the body activating the fight, flight or freeze response.

- The body may become dizzy, shakey, or it may literally crash to the floor caused by a rapid flow of blood or cortisol carried to the brain.

- Rapid breathing may occur resulting in the person feeling he or she is not getting enough oxygen, so there could be trouble breathing, which fuels the anxiety even further.

- The heart will go into overdrive and may trigger the feeling of having a heart attack, or at least cause tight chest pain.

- Some people experience a migraine as well as tightening of the muscles.

- The immune system becomes compromised which produces excessive cortisol levels as well as it presents a higher risk of developing infections.

- Sleep is often disrupted and as a result, fatigue or insomnia may set in.

- Sudden blood sugar problems could cause the brain to produce serotonin in excess and it may also create an environment for unwanted weight gain.

- Body sweats are a common side effect of anxiety.

- A lack of appetite and other tummy issues could present immediate discomforts and the potential distress of developing further digestive issues.

Some antidotes to help you manage your mind to ward off episodes of anxiety:

- Pay attention to your body & your circumstances (so you notice changes)

- Get proper nutrition, exercise and sleep - crucial habits to maintaining your health and mental well being.

- Engage in positive self talk and eliminate negative self talk. Speak well of yourself instead of putting yourself down. For example, practice saying things like: "I am trustworthy and I do my best" versus "I am not very smart and I always mess things up." Feed yourself positive affirmations and fuel your brain with nutritious healthy thoughts that produce happy results in your mindset.

- Relax and rest. Take breaks, do things you enjoy, or do mindless activities to rest your brain. Consider these suggestions: adult coloring books, gardening, doodling, listening to or playing music, sorting junk drawers, organizing a shelf in the pantry, light housework, etc. These things will give you a sense of accomplishment but not require much mental involvement. If you are experiencing anxiety, you need to give yourself permission to relax. Drinking a warm cup of chamomile or lavender tea is relaxing to the body.

- Take a hot bath or shower before bed. Essential oils in the water or in an after bath lotion will help bring calmness as you prepare to settle in for the night.

- Natural anti-stress remedies are helpful and can be found online or in health supplement stores. Do your research or ask for assistance to find what is a good option for you. Make sure that what you purchase will not interfere with any medications you may be taking. Always seek advice from your caregiver if you are taking prescription drugs.

- Turn off the extra chatter including visual chatter found on social media and television. If you are in need of renewing your mind, you might find these other sources of voices to bring confusion.

I recently heard a ministry leader say that when fear finds a way into your being, information is attracted to you that validates the lies fear has fed you. This is 100% true and I have experienced it first hand as I alluded to already. This happens because fear is fueled by an evil oppressor who is seeking to destroy and devour you. Real events and facts that are present are presented as false evidence to the lies you have listened to. Then confusion in the mind grows and causes even more anxiety because what you heard and what you believed is now coming true, at least in your mind. This is why it is important to allow the mind to take a break from the voices and chatter that will be used against you even though they may be innocent and unaware. The devil is a liar and he is sneaky but your God is truth and in Him there is no lie. He is able to dispel the lies and bring your mind back to peace but you are responsible to cooperate with Him to silence the voices that are against you. It's time to abolish anxiety and *let the peace of God which transcends all understanding, guard your hearts and your minds in Christ Jesus.*

Practice "Progressive Relaxation"…

This is a technique I was taught by Jay Jellison to command your body to release the tension it is holding. This practice helps you manage your body and control the natural response of cortisol which is carried by adrenaline that actuates our limbic system. Remember when the body feels it is in danger, it activates the limbic cycle (fight/ flight/freeze) for no apparent reason which triggers anxiety. So controlling the limbic system by way of keeping the body relaxed is a way to produce a mind over matter management system that will help you stay balanced.

Progressive Relaxation is a process of doing a "body scan relaxation" by tensing/ holding/ releasing the tension of every part of your body beginning with your feet and progressively traveling up your body to your head, then back down again. You concentrate on one area at a time and tense it up, hold the pose for five seconds, then release it and focus on the next in line area of the body to force into relaxation. You progressively "scan" your body from bottom to top and back down again. Repeat this process and then go directly to bed. I often forget to do this before bed, so once in bed with lights out, I mentally work through the technique as I tense and release my body and force it to relax. Then I go to sleep. Jay taught me this technique and I wanted to include it for you as it has been a great tool to help me. When I inquired of it with him recently, he relayed he had learned it from a counselor who had shared it with him at one time but he did not know the name of it. So I decided I would look into it later and see what I could find through research, then a few days later, I was heading into the gym to do a workout with earbuds in. As I commonly do, I will choose a YouTube video or a podcast to listen to while I do the stationary bike so I will not focus on the time, but will instead feed my mind as I exercise my body. I was shocked when Dr. Barbara Lowe, someone I had only recently discovered, began to talk about the Progressive Relaxation technique. I was watching her YouTube episode titled, "Why stability is the First Step to Wholeness with Dr. Barbara." I have since enjoyed learning from her and I want to give credit where it is due.

Further research led me to find this technique has been circling since the early 1920's, originating with Dr. Edmund Jacobson, as a way to help his patients deal with anxiety and insomnia. I want to point something out to you. I have asked the Lord to help guide every step of this process of putting this book together. When I come to a place of needing additional information, validation, or details I am missing, He has been faithful to lead me to what I need in the most random places and in the most bizarre ways. The Father is so personal and is still very creative. He gets the credit for directing my attention to the video as I guess He thought this tip was a good one to pass along. It's worth giving it a try. With that, it is time for me to say my prayers with a grateful heart, relax my body by practicing progressive relaxation myself, and get some rest.

Fear is overcome by faith so when faith arises, fear has to flee. If the root of fear is pulled up and replaced by faith, then what grows will no longer be anxiety, but will instead be a root of peace.

CHAPTER 15

GOLDEN "LEAF" NUGGETS

My prayer:

Thank you Father for providing all good things for your children and for blessing some with wisdom and knowledge beyond words, and with skills and abilities to bless others. Your Word is truth, and science is evidence of it. You desire that we all will enjoy sound minds that are free from guilt, fear, trauma, depression, anxiety, and bondage to sin. Thank you for your Word and for steps we can take to lead us to a renewed healed mind, managed by your love. Lord, teach us to intentionally fix our gaze on your face, lock eyes on your eyes and focus our thoughts on you. Fill us with your perfect peace and with your glorious presence. "You will keep in perfect peace all who trust in you, all whose thoughts are fixed on you!." Isaiah 26:3 NLT I love you so much! Suzanne

Finding wisdom is like digging up gold and I found the hidden treasure when I attended a women's conference with friends several years ago and discovered information of tremendous value. Dr. Caroline Leaf, whom I have already referred to, a communication pathologist and neuroscientist who specializes in cognitive and metacognitive neuropsychology, has authored many books of which my latest favorite is, Switch On Your Brain. I have now attended two of her conferences, have watched online teachings, and have read her books. I am a huge fan because she details the science behind how our thoughts, both good and bad, affect our brains. Dr. Leaf also teaches how your mind can literally be renewed by your thoughts, and essentially rewire your brain to replace unhealthy cells with healthy ones, thereby altering your DNA for the better. There is scientific evidence that supports what the Bible teaches and her teaching fires me up because it carries hope and physical healing with it.

I found my notes - like finding more gold ...

During the Fall of 2019, I attended another seminar and took laborious notes because I was again soaking in everything Dr. Leaf had to say. I recently ran across a notebook I had taken to the seminar and I discovered lost treasure. Now if I could only find my keys. Just kidding, but I do believe these golden nuggets I will share from my notes may be keys that will unlock something in your mind that will give you hope and will be a treasure to your heart. I give 100% credit to Dr. Caroline Leaf regarding the things I will be mentioning in this segment, according to the notes I recorded. However, if I heard or interpreted anything incorrectly as I wrote what I did not want to forget, I take full credit for the misinterpretation or misquotes. That being said, the truths of what I received not only support what I've shared in this book, according to the written Word of God, and my personal experience, but also to the scientific evidence that our awesome and mighty God is revealing to us through the Holy Spirit led experts in the field.

Please do some research for yourself. You might consider doing Dr. Caroline Leaf's *21 Day Brain Detox* program that only takes 7-10 minutes a day. It can be found online, or through the app, *Switch*. I do not receive anything from promoting Dr. Leaf, but as I have been given, I freely give. I have been given the gift of learning from her and growing my healthy mind, by her wisdom and knowledge, so I pass on to you a few quotes and hope to inspire you to seek for yourself. If you seek, you will surely find and you'll be glad you did.

Golden nuggets from my notes (from a 2019 seminar by Dr. Caroline Leaf):

- "Peace on the inside lets you rejoice in spite of your circumstances."
- "Always be in a state of renewing your mind to create a lifestyle of Mind Management."
- "Bring all thoughts into captivity and measure them against the value of love."
- "Living a life of love, power, and a sound mind is equal to living a life of renewed love. This process creates a life of prayerfulness."
- Renewing the mind = mental self care = mind management = Renewed love
- *"We have to renew our mind back to love, and the church needs to lead the way to bring the world back to love."*
- "Form deep meaningful connections with others and see people through the eyes of love by renewing our mind to love. It is required for healing of the world to take place."
- "You cannot treat the mind the same way as you do the body. The past 60 years, it has been treated the same, but it doesn't work. 99% of "who you are" is at the core of your spiritual nature. This is your Quantum nature which gives you the ability to think, feel, and choose. This "who you are" real self is made up of your spirit, your soul and your mind. 1% of "who you are" is the body and this includes the brain. Your mind and your body are separate and are not the same. As a spiritual being, that means we live 99% out of time and 1% in time in the body so we cannot treat the body and mind the same."
- "Humanity is resilient if we get our mind under control and

work as a community. Share your stories. Process through your pain. Teach people to respond instead of to react."

"The church needs to lead the way to bring the world back to love." I couldn't agree more. If we, the body of Christ do not know how to love ourselves and love others in the body, or the family of God, how can we influence the world to want the love we claim we have. It must be genuine and it begins with a transformed life, starting with the renewing of our minds. The church needs to repent of its sin of not loving one another with agape love which refers to a pure, willful, sacrificial love that intentionally desires another's highest good. I speak on behalf of the church as I have also had to repent.

Once you have been enlightened to something, it requires a response and it always has to lead us back to the heart of the Father. He IS love. As we abide in His love, He loves through us and draws others to His perfect love. He needs His children to be perfected by His love which is a greater work He accomplishes in all who are willing. If we will allow the Holy Spirit to consume us, and if we will think the thoughts of Jesus, we will be empowered to let the love of the Lord flow out of us to love the ones in front of us. We are to love our neighbors as ourselves, and I believe our neighbor is the one we are talking to, passing by, rubbing shoulders with, exchanging glances or words with and those we live by or with, work with, have a relationship with or do life with. That's just about everyone.

The year, 2020 in particular, has obviously shown us that we as a church have not done a proper job of teaching people to process through our pain, nor have we been delivered from it ourselves. We collectively do not know what to do with our feelings and thoughts, and have resorted to arguments, bullying, riots, protests and murder. *Matthew 5:21-22 NIV* addresses this, *"You have heard that it was said to the people long ago, 'You shall not murder, and anyone who murders will be subject to judgment.' But I tell you that anyone who is angry with a brother or sister will be subject to judgment..."*

The instant integration by way of social media platforms regarding the personal opinions and beliefs many feel they must express, or rather vomit on others for all to see publicly, including on those they have worshipped with, saddens my heart. As believers in Christ, we are called to a higher standard and we are to demonstrate the kindness of the Father's love with one another. *John 13:34-35 NIV* is a record of how Jesus said we are to love each other, *"A new command I give you: Love one another. As I have loved you, so you must love one another. By this everyone will know that you are my disciples, if you love one another."* Ouch!

Misinformation, misunderstandings, misinterpretations and the missing out of a Biblical values education and demonstration have all contributed to the pandemic of personal pain and lack of self-control. Most families live divided, many marriages have been destroyed and what we thought to be normal has been distracted and derailed. Do you see from a heavenly view that we have all been played? These are not the plans the Father has for us because He said according to *Jeremiah 29:11, "For I know the plans I have for you," declares the Lord, "plans to prosper you and not to harm you, plans to give you hope and a future."* The good news is there is hope for our future if we will choose to hope in Him and if we will choose to bring all our thoughts into captivity and measure them against the value of love before we speak, post or tweet.

The root of all the chaos, pain and lack of love we are witnessing is sin and because we refuse to notice it, deal with it and kill the root, we instead have chosen to kill each other with our words or with our weapons. But if we will repent and agree to entertain a new thought of love towards each other, and if we will allow the Holy Spirit to transform our lives by the renewing of our minds, and if we will turn from our sinful ways and turn our hearts to God, He promises to hear our prayers, forgive our sins and heal our land (including the landfill found deep in the heart of our minds). Individually and corporately, we need to operate with self control as we submit to the control of the Holy Spirit. Otherwise, we will remain as we are or sink further into our bondages that keep us from walking in the freedom that was bought with the highest price.

More nuggets from my Dr. Caroline Leaf seminar notes:

- *"We have to process the trauma and we have to learn to learn. The resilience inside of you is powerful but you have to activate it in order for it to work."*

- *"You have to deal with the festering root. Don't just numb something and cover it up. You have to deal with it. Don't allow shame and condemnation to steal your identity."* Your true identity is in Christ. Let Him remove the root that is keeping you bound.

- "Face the issues of life. Let the process take place. Allow the Lord to heal you as you learn to move forward. You don't get over it but you can learn to move forward past it."

- "Your genes can change by the renewing of your mind. Genes are created as the mind goes. There is hope so choose life!'

- "My thoughts influence my children from birth. We can wipe out toxic genes by renewing our minds. You can physically kill the toxic genes when you take thoughts captive and choose to renew. Your children can also be taught to renew their minds if they were born before you renewed your thoughts or were raised with your faulty beliefs."

- *"Be in the midst of whatever you're going through. Believe and walk in faith but allow God to meet you where you are. Be propelled forward."* - This reminds me of what Paul said. Put the past behind, be present in His presence and press on to what lies ahead.

- "Mental illness is not on the rise. Mismanaged minds have risen which is what has caused genes to change."

- "Don't accept labels or you will get locked in to them."

- "Trauma does not cause depression. The pain of the trauma manifests in depression but you are not clinically depressed. Depression is a response to what is happening in your environment."

Your name is NOT Depression. You do not HAVE anxiety. Do not say in agreement with the false labels statements like this: "I am depressed" or "My anxiety gets me down." When you speak this way, you speak word curses over yourself and your words become self ful-filling prophecies. This is what is meant by not aligning your thoughts with labels that define you because if you agree with your words, you tell your mind what to think. As the mind goes... your DNA goes. *"As a man thinks in his heart, so is he." Proverbs 23:7 NIV*

If your mind thinks your name is Anxiety, it will produce symp-toms of it or will fight against the body by producing DNA that agrees with the identification. You pass down thoughts in your DNA which is why you see generational diseases, or ways of life. It may have been passed to you as opposed to beginning with you and you've always wondered why you feel, think or experience things the way you do. You may be experiencing the effects of anxiety and you may feel depressed because there are some things that need to be addressed physically, mentally and I would add to it, spiritually. Trauma is very real and the effects can be debilitating. If not treated at the root and if the grief process does not take it's normal course, traumatic manifestations such as fear, anxiety, depression, etc. can be triggered long after the event with little to no warning. Though it is troubling to experience, when you are able to get freed from the cycle of trauma, you will find you have been preserved as a treasure in the process and you will be aware the Lord has come to your rescue. He adores you and He is for you.

As I shared in the chapter regarding dealing with the roots, as a reminder, the process of inner healing and receiving deliverance from this faulty DNA, may involve the need for you to repent on behalf of those who came before you. You can break the toxic DNA chain for your family and stand in the gap for generations to come. Start by asking the Holy Spirit to reveal these things to you and submit to God's plans for your life. Then, if you have been bound, you will still want to engage in the process of agreeing with new thoughts to reverse the effects you've lived with. Work with a Holy Spirit led counselor or mentor or consider doing the 21 day brain detox offered by Dr. Car-oline Leaf.

Remember these symptoms don't have you; however, you may have them residing in you, but only temporarily if you will acknowl-edge it, and go through the detoxification process to remove the toxic thoughts, receive and embrace new truthful healthy thoughts. As a result, your mind will be renewed, your brain will be rewired and your future along with the future of the generations coming behind you will be healed, restored and in alignment with who God created you to be.

Final nuggets of wisdom from my Dr. Caroline Leaf notes:

- "Change your mind, change your body. Be mindful of what you feed it. Renewing the mind is a lifestyle!"

- "Love people and help them build resilience. Strengthen each other by being there for people. Broken people need love. We were created to be consumed by love."

- "It's not easy, but be thankful for your regrets or what you have gone through. Rejoice in the realization of what you are facing. <u>When guilt, shame, condemnation or regret is brought to your mind, celebrate you are aware of it then nail it to the cross.</u> Build new thoughts and rise again."

- "Be thankful that you have learned and have been made aware of what needs to change. Use this awareness as a prompt. Be prompted to to rejoice. Choose to change."

- "It takes 21 days to break down a toxic thought and it takes 21 days to form a new thought. It takes a total of 63 days to automize and make a new habit, per new thought."

- "Get into the serious business of worshipping God and live a life of prayer-fullness."

- "Important! Don't give energy to the devil. He is defeated. Evil comes from humanity's evil use of power. We produce evil when we don't bring our thoughts into captivity."

- "Grief is not a disease. It is something you are going through because something has happened to you."

- "Recognize your feelings so you can choose well and create a proper feeling which begins the healing."

- "Detox your mind for 7-15 minutes every morning. This helps with the prevention of Alzheimer's and Dementia."

- "A state of mind carries you through the day. Put your state of mind on everyday. Be intentional about it. It only takes 15 seconds to speak truth and to speak God's words over yourself."

- *"Believe in miracles and believe that everyday is a miracle."* Remember, YOU ARE A MIRACLE.

I do believe in miracles and I do realize that my healed mind is a result of the divine supernatural miraculous work the Lord has brought me through and He is continuing to guide my steps moment by moment as I abide in Him. I know that we all have a different version of our own story and I realize there are circumstances and experiences that present unique situations that don't always lead to the exact same results. But I also believe the Word of God to be true and when we live by it, and are listening to and obeying the voice of the Holy Spirit who guides us into all truth, I believe the end result will turn out for our good and for His glory. He makes all things beautiful in His time, and He restores what was stolen or lost...even in the mind!

The good news is there is hope for our future if we will choose to hope in Him and if we will choose to bring all our thoughts into captivity and measure them against the value of love before we speak, post or tweet.

CHAPTER 16

TROUBLE, TRIBULATION AND TESTIMONY

My prayer:

Praise God You comfort my heart when I am in trouble. When trauma has overtaken me and brought tribulation to my mind, you've still been there with me and you, God, have comforted me in the middle of it. "Blessed be the God and Father of our Lord Jesus Christ, the Father of mercies and God of all comfort, who comforts us in all our <u>tribulation</u>, that we may be able to comfort those who are in any <u>trouble</u>, with the comfort with which we ourselves are comforted by God." II Corinthians 1:3-4   I love You so much, Jesus! Suzanne

Some circumstances can not be avoided or prepared for, as was the case in the accident my family experienced when I was a teenager. No amount of planning or learning could have prevented being at the intersection at the same time as a speeding vehicle driven by a drunk teenage boy who was running from the police. Some things happen because others are being negligent, revengeful or are influenced by evil or because of a freak of nature and sometimes accidents just happen. Not everything is avoidable or premeditated, yet when tragedy occurs, it usually leaves trauma in the wake of it, ready to attach itself to its victims.

According to the American Psychological Association (APA), trauma is *"an emotional response to a terrible event like an accident, rape, or natural disaster."* A person may experience trauma as a response to any event they find physically or emotionally threatening or harmful and they may feel a range of emotions. They may feel overwhelmed, helpless, shocked, or have difficulty processing their experiences. Trauma can also cause physical symptoms to manifest in the body immediately or at a later time.

There are several types of trauma as noted in a public article I read on the Medical News Today website. These different types of trauma include:

- *Acute trauma: This results from a single stressful or dangerous event.*

- *Chronic trauma: This results from repeated and prolonged exposure to highly stressful events. Ex: include cases of child abuse, bullying, or domestic violence.*

- *Complex trauma: This results from exposure to multiple traumatic events.*

- *Secondary trauma, or vicarious trauma, is another form of trauma. With this form of trauma, a person develops trauma type symptoms from close contact with someone who has experienced a traumatic event.*

It is important to be aware family members, mental health professionals, and others who care for those who have experienced a traumatic event are also at risk of experiencing vicarious trauma. The symptoms often mirror those of PTSD. If you or someone you know is in this situation, make sure you get plenty of rest, nutrition and find someone you can talk with.

If you have a prayer partner, a pastor or a close family member to stay accountable with, it would be a good idea so you can have an outlet to share your feelings and emotions as well as have someone who will look out after you and give you support. If you are unable to do these things or if you do not have this support system, it may be time to find someone else who can help care for the person you are caring for lest you both need care.

The range of symptoms resulting from trauma are wide due to many different factors, including a person's own characteristics, previous exposure to traumatic events, how they handle their emotions, and what type of traumatic episode they are experiencing. Traumatic experiences can be in the form of an isolated event or they may be a repeated, ongoing matter. A person can also experience trauma after witnessing something traumatic happening to someone else.

Trauma Trouble ...

The Emotional and psychological responses a victim of trauma experiences may include a combination of the following if not all of these symptoms: denial, anger, fear, sadness, shame, confusion, anxiety, depression, numbness, guilt, hopelessness, irritability and difficulty concentrating. They may be very emotional or may withdraw from others. Nightmares, trouble sleeping and flashbacks may also be an issue for a period of time or as a long term symptom.

Physical symptoms felt in the body are also very common with people who are suffering from trauma. They may include headaches, stomach pain or issues with digestion, insomnia, fatigue, hyperarousal (a heightened state of awareness), and other similar issues that affect the body and disrupt sleep and behavior.

I know as I stated before, that I have definitely experienced hyperarousal because I was very aware of everything going on around me. I heard every sound in and out of the home near me as all noise was amplified. When I tried to sleep, I was in an alert state of mind where I didn't feel as though I slept because my mind was racing. I was praying, thinking and processing rational and irrational thoughts all night long. I understand this irritating feeling as it is extremely hard to get a good night's sleep when you are in a state of hyper-awareness. I found a sleep aid is a good thing until you can get into a rhythm of restful sleep. (A hot bath, and a regular wind down routine is also helpful to help your body know what is coming next: sleep is the first goal.)

According to research and common knowledge, it is easy to see that a person who has suffered trauma and/or prolonged grief may also go on to develop other mental health issues, such as depression, anxiety, and substance abuse problems, though it is not always the case, and does not have to be. According to Medical News Today, *"Some research estimates that 60–75% of people in North America experience a traumatic event at some point in their life,"* and this statistic was present before the 2020 China virus worldwide pandemic. I'm curious to know what it is now as many new cases of anxiety issues have occurred. I have personally spoken to several friends who are counselors who have told me they are busier than ever. Suicide rates have risen as people have been in isolation or have experienced a fear of loss or have experienced loss of financial security, family or other traumatic events. Magazines constantly show the cover to highlight anxiety, fear and depression as their main topic.

I would say that the time is ripe to help people to find a way to be freed from living a lifetime in bondage to the effects brought upon them from grief and trauma. There is hope in Christ, though not everyone is aware of it. How will they know, unless someone tells them?

The young ones suffer most …

I was still a child, though teenagers would disagree with that statement, when I suffered the sudden loss of my mom, sister and dog at the age of 14. As I explained already, moving to a new home, school and church, as well as leaving friends, and gaining new ones along with a new first lady in our family all under a year's time, was quite traumatic. A year prior to our accident, my grandpa passed away as did two uncles. When you put this list of sudden changes all together, it is easy for me to see why I developed so much fear, need to control, and loss of many childhood memories.

Children's brains are still developing, so they are especially vulnerable to the effects of trauma. During terrible events in a child's life, they experience a heightened state of stress, and their bodies release hormones related to stress and fear. *"This type of developmental trauma can disrupt normal brain development. As a result, trauma, especially ongoing trauma, can significantly affect a child's long-term emotional development, mental health, physical health, and behavior. The sense of fear and helplessness may persist into adulthood. It leaves the person at a significantly higher risk of the effects of future trauma,"* as stated by the trauma article I read in Medical News Today, already noted. The source of the article is located at the end of the book.

Trials and tribulation ...

I can now clearly see how behaviors I carried into adulthood were attached to me as a way of self preservation and internal coping mechanisms. I had no idea until years later when all hell broke loose. I use that word because that is what it felt like when marriage trauma was added to the list. It was like someone lit a fuse and everything that had been buried, hidden and ignored came to the surface, and the pattern of anxiety and episodes of fear were put in motion.

Revelation not only carries responsibility, but it also requires a response and the ability to allow restoration to trump the tribulation brought on by sudden attacks of anxiety. When light is shed upon darkness, what is in the dark is exposed. It can be dealt with and when the darkness is deep in the soul, it can be delivered to the surface and eliminated. Then, the comfort of God is poured into those exposed places of the heart, and the Lord infuses His healing light and power into your body as a stream of peace from God fills your mind.

Healing on the Way ...

The <u>FIRST stream of healing from the hurts we receive in the world</u>, truly is to be found in the powerful living Word, who became flesh, and dwells in the flesh of all who will receive Him. Jesus Christ is my healer! He is my hope! He wants to be your healer and your hope if you will allow Him to be.

Then, as a <u>SECOND line of defense for maintaining our healing</u>, He also provides practical help because He created and inspired professionals who will walk you through the journey to wholeness. This includes a variety of treatments such as: counselors, inner healing and deliverance ministries, trauma focused therapists, programs like the 21 day brain detox by Dr. Caroline Leaf, mentors, pastors, and other accountability partners or groups that provide the type of therapy you need. Ask the Holy Spirit to guide you to the right support you need.

Your therapy may be focussed on grief and trauma, or you may need a different type of personalized therapy. It is good to seek a professional. I have done this several times and will continue periodically as a form of maintenance because sometimes things creep in we are unaware of that can be seen by another.

The goal is to remain in a state of wholeness, to manage the emotions, to prevent future episodes and to enjoy freedom from fear. It is a lifestyle of love, joy, peace, patience, kindness, gentleness, goodness, faithfulness and self control that we will experience as we continue to dwell in the presence of God. It is this place where we reside with a spirit of love, power and a sound mind. Our minds and our hearts are guarded when we abide in His rest and in His Word. It is this place of abiding rest I like the best.

Habits towards maintaining wellness and healing ...

In addition to inner spiritual healing, and the help of personalized trauma therapy, it is good to include habits that provide your body with the help it needs to attain and stay healthy. Practicing self-care can help you cope with the emotional, psychological, and physical symptoms of trauma.

Exercise: Since trauma can activate the body's fight-flight-freeze response, exercise may help alleviate some of these effects.

Practice mindfulness: Be in the present. Speak the truth of what you know to be true. Remind yourself of reality when your mind is focussed on irrational thoughts. Write out your feelings and thoughts, or close your eyes and imagine Jesus sitting in front of you. Speak words of peace outloud and practice being in His presence. Remember, He will keep in perfect peace, the one whose mind is stayed on Him. Focus on Jesus and activate your faith over the fear you are experiencing. It is NOT your fear and it does NOT belong to you. Tell fear to leave while you remain in peace.

Connect with others: Withdrawal from others is a common symptom of trauma. However, connecting with friends and family is important. According to the Anxiety and Depression Association of America, staying in contact with people can help to prevent trauma from becoming PTSD. Isolation for a short period may be helpful to the traumatized person, but helping him or her, or yourself, to engage with others can improve your mood and your well-being. If you feel comfortable talking about the trauma with someone you trust, allow it to happen and see how it makes you feel. If you are unable to share details of your experience, just let your friend or family member know you just want them to be near you as a companion at the moment. You can engage in your own activities like reading, a hobby, an adult coloring book, sitting in silence, listening to music, going for a walk or a bike ride, or whatever you want to do. The point is that we need each other, the human touch and intimacy. Human interaction is a gift to our hearts and a guide in our healing.

Maintain a balanced lifestyle: Get a good night's sleep (7-9 hours), eat a nutritious diet, exercise, and do activities you enjoy. Avoid drugs and alcohol and limit your caffeine. Make sure to laugh often and love freely.

Say your prayers, thank your caregivers and be grateful: Gratefulness prepares your heart to receive your healing that is on the way!

Trauma, troubles and tribulation may have taunted you for a time, and they may have left you feeling stuck in your hurts that the world has hurled at you, but lift up your eyes because hope lies just ahead of you. Grief truly is good when we grow through it and as we climb out of it. One step at a time, we take a leap of faith and then suddenly realize we have reached a new height and are healed. "Good grief," I tell my soul. I was hurt by worldly circumstances, but God healed my heart and my mind by the power of His Word. His Word brings healing in its wings.

The word of their testimony ...

I decree and declare that God is faithful and true and in Christ alone I will boast. He is my hope and He is my salvation. My righteousness is His righteousness and it is by the indwelling power of the Holy Spirit dwelling in my heart that I am free to forgive, love, live and remain in a state of healing. There is no name higher than the name of Jesus Christ, the resurrected Savior. I am a daughter of the Most High God, and He is my Father. I am eternally grateful for the treasures found in trauma and the good gifts produced through grief. The devil came to kill, steal and destroy, but I am dancing in the overflow of hope, peace and joy. He tried to kill my marriage, but we are approaching thirty-three years and are more in love than ever. We are faithful and we are thankful because Jesus restored our holy matrimony and re-wrote our HIStory. I serve a mighty God and I will never stop. I am an overcomer by the blood of the Lamb, the word of my testimony and that I am not afraid of losing my life. You see, on the day I leave my earthly tent in death, I will be completely healed and fully alive. In Christ I live and in Christ I hope. God gave me His healing Word as a legal and binding promissory note and I'm taking it to the bank!

> *Grief truly is good when we grow through it and as we climb out of it. One step at a time, we take a leap of faith and then suddenly realize we have reached a new height and are healed.*

REFERENCED RESOURCES

Christy Austin, MA, LPCC, Founder, Healing Talk LLC [healing-talk.online] President, Enkindle Ministries [enkindleministries.com]

Dr. Barbara Lowe: "Why Stability is the First Step to Wholeness with Dr. Barbara" YouTube Link: [https://youtu.be/fPH02rxcqU0]

Dr. Carolina Leaf: "5 Steps to Identify & Eliminate the Root of Anxiety or Any Mental Illness Health Issue" YouTube Link: https://youtu.be/xkRQyhGYUnc]

Enkindle Ministries [enkindleministries.com] – Greg and Suzanne Grimaud serve this national ministry to transform the nation with His Presence, one community at a time. Greg is the Director of the Linked Business Network. The couple serves as City Taker Hub leaders.

Evangelist Jay Jellison, BecomingLoveMinistries.com (Inner Healing and DeliveranceMinistries) and IronAcresRanch.com (family gatherings, spiritual renewal, staff retreats)

FamilyID – Greg Gunn Explore the website @ family-id.com

Pastor Jay Pike message, "Surrounded by Mercy" The Gate Church, Nov. 15, 2020 Link: https://youtu.be/6LNcjS4kLuQ <Based on Ps. 32. Forward to Min. 55:05>

Rev. Daniel Palmer, Licensed marriage and Family Counseling: Inquire about physical or virtual counseling by email danieloutofden@gmail.com

SOURCES OF BIBLIOGRAPHY

Blue Letter Bible, online study tool, https://www.blueletterbible.org/ (also found through the app store)

Buckley, Dylan, Medically Reviewed By: Deborah Horton, "Understanding The Stages Of Grief," BetterHelp.com, Updated November 19, 2020, https://www.betterhelp.com/advice/grief/understanding-the-stages-of-grief/

Goldman, Rena. "What is Jacobson's Relaxation Technique?" Healthline.com, Updated on July 21, 2020, Medically reviewed by Timothy J. Legg, Ph.D., CRNP. https://www.healthline.com/health/what-is-jacobson-relaxation-technique

Harvard Health Publishing, "Understanding the Stress Response," Updated: July 6, 2020, https://www.health.harvard.edu/staying-healthy/understanding-the-stress-response

Heid, Markham, "How to Help a Friend or Loved One," Time Magazine, an updated reissue of Time's Special Edition, Display till 9/11/20, Mental Health, A New Understanding

Leaf, Caroline, Dr., website store: https://drleaf.com/collections/all Book referenced: "Switch On Your Brain"

24-7prayer.com, "Prayer Tool: Identificational Repentance" pdf, https://downloads.24-7 prayer.com/prayer_course/2019/resources/pdfs/26%20Identificational%20Repentance.pdf

Leonard, Jayne, "What is trauma? What to know" Medical News Today, Last medically reviewed on June 3, 2020, https://www.medicalnewstoday.com/articles/trauma#summary

Mirgain, Shilagh, PhD and Singles, Janice PsyD. "Progressive Muscle Relaxation" (2016). A collaborative effort between the University of Wisconsin Integrative Health Program, VA Office of Patient

Centered Care and Cultural Transformation, and Pacific Institute for Research and Evaluation. https://wholehealth.wisc.edu/tools/progressive-muscle-relaxation/

Seltzer, Leon F., PhD., "Trauma and the Freeze Response: Good, Bad, or Both?" Psychology Today, Posted Jul 08, 2015 https://www.psychologytoday.com/us/blog/evolution-the-self/201507/trauma-and-the-freeze-response-good-bad-or-both

Streit, Jonathan. "Is a Limbic System Impairment Hijacking Your Health?" Institute for Restorative Health, July 30,   2020. https://instituteforrestorativehealth.com/2020/07/29/is-the-limbic-system-hijacking-your-health/

❤ *Suzanne*

**To connect with Suzanne Grimaud and
to access additional resources,
visit the Author's website
@ SuzanneGrimaud.com
or by email: SuzanneGrimaudSpeaks@gmail.com**

Request Suzanne to be your podcast or webinar guest or to enjoy a live or virtual media conversation. Consider having her speak or minister to your group at your next live or online event, gathering or retreat.

Have a personal healing testimony or story of your own? Share it with the author! Let's celebrate the goodness of God, together! Visit the Author website to communicate.

Would you like someone to pray for you? Suzanne loves to do that too. Send a message to her through SuzanneGrimaud.com. You may also request prayer through the national prayer line

@ EnkindleMinistries.com, which Suzanne and her husband, Greg, are actively involved with.

FIND THE REST OF THE STORY
not shared in this book...
@ SuzanneGrimaud.com

"Forgiveness ~ Its A Choice" – MP3 Audio Testimonies
Greg & Suzanne Grimaud (2008 original recording)

Full testimony to offer hope for marriages. Listen online.

True Story: Forgiveness & Restored Marriage – Video
Trinity Broadcast Network.

June, 2016 TBN Video interview with Greg & Suzanne Grimaud.

Social Connections may be found on the Author Website!

THE CEDAR GATE
FOR GENERATIONS JOURNEY
Stewarding Your Story

Write your legacy book!

For Generations Journey is a three day experience getting your stories and values out of your head and into print.

IMPACT FUTURE GENERATIONS
Take the time to leave your written story
that will last through the ages.

YOUR VALUES AND VIRTUES
As you share your story, your values
and virtues will shine through.

EXPRESS YOUR FAITH
Document your spiritual journey and
the impact it has had in your life.

CAST A VISION
Put in writing what you would like to
see future generations accomplish.

AGENDA
Enjoy 3 days in a luxury cabin.
Spend time with like-minded people.
Work with an experienced coach.
Build a detailed timeline of your life.
Create chapter outlines.
Audio record chapters.
Transcribe audio files.
Develop rough manuscript.

TheCedarGate.com
randy@thecedargate.com
405-474-0078

CEDAR GATE
PUBLISHING

THE
CEDAR GATE
CONNECTING → IMPACTING → GENERATIONS